MARY WIGMAN    THE LANGUAGE OF DANCE

# Mary Wigman  The Language of Dance

Translated from the German by WALTER SORELL

Photographs by Charlotte Rudolph

WESLEYAN UNIVERSITY PRESS : MIDDLETOWN, CONNECTICUT

The German edition of this work, titled *Die Sprache des Tanzes,*
was published, copyright © 1963, by Ernst Battenberg Verlag,
Stuttgart
ISBN 0-8195-6037-5
Library of Congress Catalog Card Number: 66–18118
Manufactured in the United States of America
First paperback edition, 1974

# Contents

MARY WIGMAN    THE LANGUAGE OF DANCE

MARY WIGMAN

PORTRAIT BY JOSEPH BENKERT

WITCH DANCE I    1914

# The Secret of the Dance

My friends want me to write a book. They say it ought to be the "book of my life." What should I tell? My life? Life, fully lived, is a rounded thing. It is better to let it be and to let it complete its course instead of cutting it into small pieces like a birthday cake.

Today I am an old woman and, except for some physical complaints which burden everyday life, a happy old woman. And this is the time of the "little" happiness. It is wonderful to sit at one's desk quietly, to reflect and give one's thoughts a playful freedom which lets them slide into dreams, and to follow with one's eyes as far as one would follow the tiny blue cloudlings of cigarette smoke.

Suddenly I think of Marcel Marceau, of that wonderful study of his in which, in a minute's time, he demonstrates human life in its changing stages:

Youth — maturity — old age — death.

I have experienced them all, the seasons of life, and I am now gliding into the phase at the exit of which Death waits for us all as the final crowning of our lives. I am not afraid of him. Because whenever I have encountered him with his imperious bearing or with his dark, impatiently threatening gesture, he has always been surrounded by the magnificence of farawayness and the majesty of those silent unfathomabilities which make us bow to them even when, torn by pain, we feel at their mercy. I know fear; perhaps it is a fear of what precedes death, of sickness and lingering illness and of becoming a burden to other people. But this, too, we have to bear, as we have borne so many things in life which were not less difficult to face and yet had to be overcome. This last time, however, it will be accepted with the consoling awareness that — finally! — we need not start all over again.

God only knows, it *was* wonderful always to have to begin again and to be able to start anew. I would not wish to have missed anything that life took from me and gave me. Even the mistakes I have made I cannot regret. Because life always presents its bill in the end. And one has to pay it in full. No, I am not afraid of death. Is he not the most faithful companion of old age and his hour the last act of purification one has to go through?

I look in the mirror. It shows me the face of my age, scored with wrinkles and wrinklets, furrowed and familiar like a landscape in which one has found oneself and no longer asks whether one likes it or not. Every experience has left a trace behind it. Again and again the present has covered the previous imprint, layer upon layer, putting everything in its right place. It is strange to think that even my face now will have to change again. And if I should live to see it, what will the face of the very old woman be like?

Well, here I am sitting at my desk trying to decide what I should report. To live, to experience happens once only. To look back into the past, to let it emerge again as memory, means to see it through the mirror of the present and, from this point of view, to put the image into its frame. I have always been a fanatic of the present, in love with the moment. Hence it is not easy for me to recall life's images, visions, and happenings.

My friends, shall I tell you the story of the ugly duckling that miraculously turned into a swan? Because it could not be foreseen that the mousy little girl would be transformed into a world-famous dancer. This certainly may seem a metamorphosis bordering on the miraculous. But to me this process of growing did not seem so miraculous. It took too long, was too difficult and with all its deviations nevertheless too consistent. Of course, I love to talk and to tell stories. When sitting at my desk, image upon image wells up in me and I can easily imagine that rather amusing, colorful memoirs would result. But is this my task? I am not a writer, and I would never be able to invent a plot, peopled by characters and full of situations deserving any literary acclaim. There has always been only one theme around which my thoughts circled like moths around a light: *Dance*.

The medium of creativity granted me was the dance, always and ever the dance. Therein I could invent and create. Therein I have found my poetry, have given shape and profile to my visions, have molded and built, toiled and worked on the human being, with the human being, and for the human being. It might very well be that I love the dance so immensely because I love life, because of its metamorphoses and elusiveness. Time and again I have felt enraptured by its "die and arise." To face life the way it approaches us, even to approve of it when it appears unbearable, to remain true to oneself and to obey "the law that called us into being," to help accomplish the predestined changes of time, space, and form in ourselves — isn't all this the process of growing which we have to follow? To live life and to affirm it in the creative act, to elevate and glorify it? That is what I want to write about. For you, my friends; for you, my students; for you who will come after me; and for all of you who love the dance. And even if the danced message, in the uniqueness of its form-turned-revelation, defies capture in the spoken or written word — because it has no need for words — even then one may convey something of that pure and profound bliss with which man is blessed when, in moments of full awareness of his being, he opens and shapes the realms of his experience. In the same way as I have tried during my entire life to fuse personality and work, I have attempted to open roads for my pupils leading deep within themselves and to bring them to the point where knowledge and divination become oneness, where experience and creativity penetrate each other. And as I now try to retrace and re-create with verbal images some of the most important stages of my work, the result is not going to be a textbook. Nevertheless, it may have something to say to some of you and may help you to come closer to the meaning of the dance. Its secret? That lies hidden in the living breath which is the secret of life.

# The Language of Dance

The dance is a living language which speaks of man — an artistic message soaring above the ground of reality in order to speak, on a higher level, in images and allegories of man's innermost emotions and need for communication. It might very well be that, above all, the dance asks for direct communication without any detours. Because its bearer and intermediary is man himself, and because his instrument of expression is the human body, whose natural movement forms the material for the dance, the only material which is his own and his own to use. This is why the dance and its expression are so exclusively bound to man and his ability to move. Where this ability ceases to be, the dance faces the limitations of its creative and performing possibilities.

This seems so little! And yet in this littleness lies the language of the dance in all its manifold forms which can be changed anew time and again. Certainly, bodily movement alone is not yet dance. But it is the elemental and incontestable basis without which there would be no dance. When the emotion of the dancing man frees the impulse to make visible his yet invisible images, then it is through bodily movement that these images manifest themselves in their first stages. And it is movement through which the projected dance gesture receives the living breath of its rhythmically pulsating power.

Movement gives meaning and significance to the artistically shaped and formed gesture-language. For the dance becomes understandable only when it respects and preserves its meaning relative to the natural movement-language of man. Beyond the personal interpretation underlying the dancer's gesture, there is always the responsibility and obligation to make clear the universal, super-personal meaning — which the dancer can neither change forcibly nor exchange arbitrarily without endangering the general validity of his message. Also in the dance I cannot call the earth heaven, if I mean the earth.

The same way as music, dance too is called an "art of time." This holds true as long as one refers to the measurable, countable rhythmic passages which can be controlled in time. But that's not all! It would be little else but stale theory were we to determine the rhythm of the dance solely from the element of time. True, counting is spelled with capital letters by us dancers. We need it especially in our choreographic work, during the process of creation and the rehearsing of group works in the modern dance or ballet. We need it as an expediency to account for the structure of the two cooperating artistic languages, dance and music, to attune them to each other in their temporal course and bring them together in harmonious understanding. We need it to define the beats, to clarify the transitions from one theme to the next, to be precise in giving the necessary accents, the moments of arrested movement and breathing. There is always counting. The musicians count and the dancers count. And sometimes they miss one another in counting, because the musicians count along the musical line whereas the dancers arrive at their counting through the rhythm of movement.

In the same manner as time, if not even more compellingly, the element of strength plays its part in the dance — the dynamic force, moving and being moved, which is the pulsebeat of the life of dance. One could also call it the living breath of dancing. For breath is the mysterious great master who reigns unknown and unnamed behind all and everything — who silently commands the function of muscles and joints — who knows how to fire with passion and to relax, how to whip up and to restrain — who puts the breaks in the rhythmic structure and dictates the phrasing of the flowing passages — who, above and beyond all this, regulates the temper of expression in its interplay with the colorfulness of rhythm and melody. Of course, this has nothing in common with a normal breathing method. The dancer must be able to breathe in every one of his stances and situations. He is then hardly aware of his organic breathing; he is ruled by the law of his dynamically propelled power of breathing which reveals itself in the momentary degree of its intensity and strain. When the dancer crosses through space with solemnly measured steps, his deep and calm breathing gives his carriage and movement an appearance of innermost composure and completion in itself; and when — by incessantly springing up and down — he throws himself into a condition of flickering agitation which not only takes possession of his body but of the entire being, then there no longer exists a moment of quiet breathing for him. He breathes, rather, with the same vibration that fills and shakes his whole being.

There is hardly another dance movement in which the power of dynamic breathing, increasing effect and accomplishment, is felt as strongly as in the leap. When the dancer starts to jump, he chases the stream of his breath like lightning from below to the top, from the feet upward through the body, to be able to hold his breath from the instant of leaving the ground until he has reached the height of his leap and has almost gone beyond it. In these few seconds of his utmost exertion, holding his breath, he actually defies all gravity, becomes a creature of the air, and seems to fly or float through space. At the downcurve only, his breath flows back into the relaxing body and returns the dancer to the earth after his short soaring flight.

Time, strength, and space: these are the elements which give the dance its life. Of this trinity of elemental powers, it is space which is the realm of the dancer's real activity, which belongs to him because he himself creates it. It is not the tangible, limited, and limiting space of concrete reality, but the imaginary, irrational space of the danced dimension, that space which can erase the boundaries of all corporeality and can turn the gesture, flowing as it is, into an image of seeming endlessness, losing itself in self-completion like rays, like streams, like breath. Height and depth, width and breadth, forward, sideward, and backward, the horizontal and the diagonal — these are not only technical terms or theoretical notions for the dancer. After all, he experiences them in his own body. And they become his living experience because through them he celebrates his union with space. Only in its spatial embrace can the dance achieve its final and decisive effect. Only then the fleeting signs are compressed into a legible and lasting mirror image in which the message of the dance grows into what it should and must be: language — the living, artistic language of dance.

And now let's lower our voice and be a bit wary! For we want to enter the realm of creativity, the space in which the hidden form and the seeking form circle one another, intertwine and wait in the twilight of their dream for the light to come in order to give them color and contours and to illuminate what has turned into an "image." Whoever would be brash enough to enter here with the blazing torch of curiosity would find little more than a mistily drifting cluster of images. For this space does not permit a direct approach. It does not respond to concrete demands. It does not yet know of structure, it knows neither name nor number. It does not want to yield to anything, it does not heed commands. It is the space of creative readiness and is a sanctuary. Therefore, let us lower our voice and listen to the pulsebeat of our heart, to the whisper and murmur of our own blood, which is the sound of this space. This sound wants to become song! But its wings are still tied, it lacks the strength to unfold them and to speak in its upward flight. Thus it sinks back into the space of twilight depth, sucks in its own powers, and returns, heavy with dreams and images, into the realm in which it may be comprehended and may yield to form.

Creative ability belongs to the sphere of reality as much as to the realm of fantasy. And there are always two currents, two circles of tension, which magnetically attract one another, flash up and oscillate together until, completely attuned, they penetrate one another: on the one hand, the creative readiness which evokes the image; on the other hand, the will to act whipped up to a point of obsession, that will which takes possession of the image and transforms its yet fleeting matter into malleable working substance in order to give it its final form in the crucible of molding.

12

To compose means to build. A work of art does not come to its creator in his sleep, ready made. The theme for the dance can occur to the dancer in the scuffle and shuffle of the street as well as under the wide open sky. The idea, even in its invention, is a gift! But the work of art is creation, is the artistic deed for which the creator is responsible as much as it is testimony to his being.

There are not only the intoxicating moments of conceiving the image. There also is an ecstasy of sober work.

How many works are left unborn! Perhaps because the "blessed" minute was missed — perhaps also because the form-giving will tired too quickly, or because the image in the imagination was yet too pale and vague to be molded into substance and theme. Even when we, intoxicated with creativeness, believe ourselves near the realization of our conception — so near that it seems to need only one more breath to capture it definitely — it still may happen that the splendor of its glowing cascades scatters and the kindled light in ourselves becomes a will-o'-the wisp, luring us, seducing us, misleading us . . . until it goes out.

However, have I not felt, seen, and experienced all of it? I was filled with it, for days, weeks, and months! It was with me through the night and did not let go of me during the day. It was always there and clandestinely ever present. I never talked to anyone about it. Like a precious jewel I carried it with me in myself, protecting it from any disturbing touch. Was all this deception only? Where was I to begin, how was I to decide? And if the first tentative try should not succeed, what then? Would I keep up my courage in spite of that, would I be able to do it in spite of that? One doubts and despairs of everything, even at last of oneself, and in the end one carries it off nevertheless. For there is a power which does not cease to urge on, and there is a voice which cannot be quieted: You have to — you have to — ! And don't you also *want* to? Is this pushing and driving, this wrestling and battling, not your greatest glory, not your greatest passion? — "I do not let go of thee, unless thou blesseth me."

It may happen that image and form, experience and structure, inflame one another like lightning and so entirely penetrate one another that the execution and completion of the work do not encounter any hurdle. But in most cases the opened flow of the dance material is still too confusing in its tumbling abundance to permit a solidified and final compositional form without friction. And if it comes off — if the content-and-theme-fused idea holds up in the sober light of the studio, if the idea is rounded off in its shape and completed as a composition — nevertheless the final version never quite lives up to the original image. There is always something left to be desired between the conceived work and the one emerging from its creator, and a little drop of woefulness is mixed with the pure bliss of creating.

Alas, there is the fearful question during the process of working: Will it succeed? Will it be this time, this one time, quite perfect? And if it will be surrendered to the public as the confession it is, can it stand up to that trial by fire? As long as it is within the sphere of the workshop, it is under my protection and invulnerable! But when the last step has been taken, when the final gesture writes its *finis* and I must not change anything any more and must be satisfied with what I have accomplished — then not only do I face the form-fulfilled work, but also the original image calls me to account: "What have you made of me? Shrouded in a hundred veils I came to you. They all had their meaning. Have you woven them into your woof and warp, which should have turned into my image, into my mirror reflection? Did it become this mirror image?" And if the answer would be a hesitant or even unconcerned "Yes" — if it had to be "Yes" because the newborn creature of fantasy wanted to live, should live, and — perhaps — could live — behind all this, however, would still lurk the deeper awareness: Imperfect — unfinished — this time too.

On the other hand, the knowledge that every created work is always no more than a step on the way to perfection, but can never be perfection itself, is not really painful. Because out of a yet deeper within-ness emerges a certainty of the continuity of all creative powers which will rekindle themselves when attempting the next task, and they will stand the test and prove themselves. Before the gate to the paradise of ultimate perfection stands the angel with the flaming sword; in his magnificent uncorruptibility, he refers every human being bidding for entrance to his proper place. We should say thanks for it! For his refusal protects us from the wretchedness of stupid self-satisfaction and vanity, from the satiation of a contentment too easily arrived at, and from illusions of grandeur. The striving for perfection is innate with every artistically creative person and accompanies him through all phases of his life and work. To him, it is propelling force and admonishment, signpost and goal. Certainly I can reach a goal set by myself. But it is always one goal only, a passing-through; never the last and ultimate.

If we were gods or even supermen, we would not need to strive for perfection. We would possess it from the very beginning and would not be aware of it at all. But was ever a human being permitted to cross the threshold separating him from the unimaginable lofty room of his completion in perfection? We do not know. Our imagination has not yet been able to create a visible and valid image for this room. How should it be possible for us to breathe, to live, and moreover to work in it?

Our stars glow for us from afar and out of darkness. Aren't they a thousand times more beautiful, more alluring and mysterious, because they are unattainable? What would artistic creativeness mean if there were no yearning, no far-reaching, dreamlike longing which does not permit us to tarry and opens the path to movement in which, ever transfigured, it renews itself time and again?

We called Goethe the "Olympian" and said of Beethoven that he was a titan. This moves them into the proximity of the godlike. In spite of it they have remained humans, and their work is not administered by the gods but is committed to our very human care. We even bestowed human features on the gods and Prometheus who, in full consciousness of his procreating strength, arrogantly assumed that he had the power of emulating the gods and was denied the fulfillment of perfect achievement. There are so many moving and magnificent images, so many poetic and philosophical examples bearing witness to the eternal yearning of man for the expression of perfection. And we have never ceased to ask questions. But the closer our questions come to the roots of all things, the more sparing and hesitant do they become. And no man has yet found for his fellowmen an answer to the ultimate questions.

For at the gate to the paradise of highest perfection, there the angel still stands with flaming sword refusing entry. And by his side there is the benevolent genie of man, with an inexplicable smile, putting his finger to his lips: Up to here and no further. Without the secret, what would all artistic creation be? Why was not the creative power equally distributed among all men? Why do only a few feel themselves to be called and why are even fewer chosen? The secret! One has to accept it and to bow to it. In the secret, however, lives the promise. — And if creative man would have felt only a passing breath of it in a few fulfilled hours of his long life span, I believe he would be blessed.

# Forms of Dance

The dance belongs to the performing arts. In its theatrical reality, dance depends on its legitimate interpreter, the dancer. And just as he is able to express himself only in the short moments of his live performance, so is the artistic realization of the dance limited in time and bound to the moment. With the fall of the curtain, not only does the power of projection of the dance performance vanish, but the work itself seems to dissipate and to fade from the eyes of the spectator. True, one can hold onto it in a film. But even then it is little more than a weakened repetition of its scenic sequence. In order to visualize it afterward in its concept and structural composition, one cannot look it up in a book or script as one does with a play, or in a score or its arrangement for the piano as one does with an opera. The dance work immediately turns into an image of memory which can be conjured up and preserved only to a certain degree; it vanishes more quickly or more slowly, depending on the level of the work and the quality of its performance.

I have often been asked whether it is not painful to me to experience the evanescence of my own dance works. Well, after all, I can look back on an impressive number of self-composed and successfully performed solo dances, dance cycles, group dances, choreographies for stage and choric dance works, but I must admit that I have never really mourned their loss. They simply became part of the past! Their fleeting uniqueness, which they received in the process of creation — their transience, so basic to the dance itself — have always seemed to me to have been conditioned and dictated by its nature. For instance, I would never have wanted to perform the dances of my youth again later in life and probably would never have been able to do so, because different and more essential things have taken their places in the various seasons of my life which made it unnecessary, in fact superfluous, to turn back to the past.

Dance wants to and has to be seen. Only when seen can it become a feast to the eye and, in its ultimate perfection, a moving, enchanting, and beguiling experience. I don't have to stress the fact that the first prerequisite for such a sweeping and compelling impact is the talent for dancing — a gift of nature which may be aroused, encouraged, and developed, but which cannot be forced, let alone created. Nor do I have to say that one must have learned one's craft thoroughly and must master it, all the more since the demands of body and technique imposed upon the dancer are exceedingly great. Of course, wherever technique is worshipped for its own sake, art ceases to be. Terpsichore covers her head and silently turns away from the child of her love, from then on refusing him the grace of her gift.

Dance talents and their varied shadings are manifold. In general, there are two recognizable kinds of talents, namely the creative and the instrumental talent.

The ideal case would be the one in which both talents coincide in one human being whose creative fantasy, structural sense, masterly technique, and compelling ability to perform would find a self-willed expression and style in his personal artistic handwriting. In the dance, too, the adage concerning the many who feel the calling and of the few who are chosen holds true. After all, there are only the few towering personalities, the truly gifted and blessed, who, through the accomplishments of their living creativity, give the dance the stimulation for renewing its content and contribute, time and again, to the ever necessary changing of form and style.

Looking back on the history of the European dance, we see in each of its epochs the names of the great and greatest dancers and choreographers — glowing like stellar constellations — at least from the time when dance was accepted as an art form. Their accomplishments, powerful in their momentary impact and at the same time pregnant with their projection into the future, became exemplar and measuring rod, often for many a generation. And yet again the traditional heritage had to be shaken and taken apart whenever a dance personality appeared who knew how to give a familiar image the new face of its own time.

There are ingeniously gifted dancers who find their strongest fulfillment in the solo dance. This means neither poorness nor limitation. At best, it shows that they do not have the gift of pouring their creative powers into all those ramified channels from which the larger forms of the dance are fed. But what riches the blessed soloist has to offer! How much enchantment he may convey if he can build up his program to a rapturous and scenically brilliant delivery! The solo dance is the most condensed form of the danced message. Whether the character of his theme is dramatic or gay and playfully funny, whether abstractly formulated or pantomimically defined, whether contemplative or resigned, whether intensely jubilant or deadly sad — there always seems to be enacted something like a dialogue for the spectator, a dialogue in which the dancer holds a conversation with himself and with an invisible partner.

I have experienced this kind of completely irrational partnership a hundred times within myself, and every time I was fascinated by it again and again. I have very often asked myself what this partnership consists of and what brings it forth. In some of my dances, as, for instance, in *Dialogue* or *Love Song*, it was clear from the beginning that I turned to an invisible but in my imagination absolutely present partner, namely to the ideal lover who took the place of the real lover. The partnership was also clear in *Dialogue with a Demon*. But there were other themes and more abstract forms where it was not so easily recognizable, and yet it was there.

Within the framework of a solo dance cycle whose six dances were put together under the heading of *Sacrifice* was the dance *Death Call*. At the conception of this dance I did not start with the image of death by any means! This relation — and with it the title — was only established in the last stages of its choreographic birth. But there was from the very beginning something like a feeling of "being called" that came from afar, emerging from a deep darkness and relentlessly demanding. It forced the glance of my uplifted eyes to turn toward the depths and made me spread out my arms like a barrier which rose up against an onrushing power. I wanted to storm forward, to throw myself against this power! But already after the first few steps I had to stop as if transfixed. There a halt was put to it which almost hit me like a magic command.

What was it, who was it, who called me and made me stop? A voice? A figure? A thing remembered? Nothing like that at all. But there it was, an opposite pole, a point in space, arresting eye and foot. This probably self-created and space-reflected tension, however, forced the body into a sudden turn and twisted my back down into a deep bend in which the arms spread out again, helpless and hopeless this time. Now it hovered over me, this power, and widened into an immense shadow which permitted no escape. But no weakness either! For I did not really intend to withdraw from it; on the contrary, I wanted to penetrate it, I wanted to understand, comprehend, experience. Tremendously large black banners began to fly and to rustle. They were neither sinister nor threatening. They were of a sober, swinging magnitude; to the rhythm of these banners the once arrested feet could begin to unshackle themselves and move sweepingly in a sequence of big steps. Thus the dance unfolded in a succession of static, monumental poses and hugely conceived movements through space.

Question and answer! But they spoke from within me simultaneously. I became the "caller" and the "called" all in one. At a certain point of the dance I began to shiver. And I suddenly knew: Death is speaking to you. Not my death, nor the death of any other human being. It was rather as if a law of life wanted to be enforced, a command I had never encountered before. And a first knowledge grew within me of all that was hidden behind life, the first realization of all irrevocabilities, of all finality and extinction. And that is how

DEATH CALL

IGOR STRAVINSKY

THE RITES OF SPRING

the dance ended in the conscious acceptance and recognition of that great law that looms above all of us and that we call Death.

This invisible partnership is also effective in the pantomimic dance and even then remains the same when it experiences a certain definition of milieu and situation through the metamorphosis of the dancer, through his embodiment of a clearly drawn and closely circumscribed character. At that moment, however, in which the imaginary partner takes shape and faces the dancer as a reality, the duet, the *pas de deux,* is being born. It shifts the dance event onto a level of plot and casts the various partners — now in a personified counterpart — in roles growing out of the action. Of course, this visual partnership need not be limited to the duet. It can be expanded into all forms, from the solo recital to dance works employing large groups.

The majority of all dancers have interpretive talent, can be used like instruments. Although their creative potentialities may be limited, for the choreographer and director they are the most valuable plastic material, the ideal instruments of expression in which the molding of his dance ideas can find the clearest mirror reflection. Something strangely exciting happens during the direct communication from man to man, from the dance creator to the dancing performer. Although the given form remains the same, although its content is in no way changed, nevertheless it undergoes a transfiguration in the interpretive reflection of the performer! It is like an echo, which also returns our call word for word. Only the timbre has changed, and it seems to reach us from another dimension. Like it, the creative idea also changes in its instrumental re-creation by the dancer and becomes a purely performing property to such a degree that it can make us forget its original authorship.

How often have I experienced this fascinating process! How often have I suffered when my own ideas remained behind the promises of their conception — but how often did I also rejoice when I saw that they were heightened in their danced performance. I am deeply grateful to the many dancers who have worked with me in the course of my long creative life. For they were and still are the ones who help to form the very existence of the choreographic notions — and only justify the work as such through their dedicated and inspired performance.

Also the choreographic work — the invention, the shaping and rehearsing of group works — requires a special talent. In spite of possessing this gift myself, I hardly know how to analyze it. Is it the inner vision in which the theme presents itself? Is it thinking in terms of movement in space? The creative pleasure of sculpturing the moving figures which populate the space? Or is it simply the challenge of a given task, the stimulation through the chosen music which evokes the creative urge? Oh — this so often confounded and yet so very much loved compelling urge to create which sometimes clandestinely lies in ambush like a wild beast, to attack one at the very moment one expects it least!

In ninety-nine out of a hundred cases the choreographer is author and director in one person. His task demands: to design, to plan, to build — and this always with regard to the work's effectiveness on stage, to its re-creation through the dancing human beings who, under his leadership, turn into an orchestra of moving bodies. In wrestling with idea and form, in judging the opposing forces that result, therein lies the true accomplishment of the choreographer. The fanaticism of his artistic will compels him to overcome these difficulties. And the finished work gives him an almost humble happiness which finds its crowning glory in the performance of his dance.

Solo dance — group dance — choric dance: these are the three great complexes of expression and form in which the dance unfolds and is effective. As species they are, no doubt, distinguishable from one another. But they are by no means always distinguishable as to their themes.

This, too, I have experienced more than once. For instance, the theme *wandering* I have created in a threefold variation: once as a solo dance with the idea of the fateful road of a lonesome man; a second time as group dance with the thought of many individuals, differing from one another but meeting on their independently started journeys and joining on the road ahead; and a third and last time as a choric event which, in its symbolism, refers to the experiences of war, especially of the post-war period — to the fate of homelessness which sends all of them together on their sad wandering and which is to be endured only because of the unshakable belief in the ineradicable promise of a new home and new roots. Neither the number of the dancers nor the theme itself determines the choreographic form. It is rather the inmost feeling and approach of the dance creator which gives the work its ultimate character.

When I received the assignment to give Stravinsky's *Le Sacre du printemps* — *The Rites of Spring* — its stage image, I was delighted. For I loved this music more than anything else, and also the theme seemed to conform with my creative potentialities. I admit I was warned about the difficulties of this work and its past choreographic failures. But what does this mean when one is "possessed"? And so I started enthusiastically with the work, invented characters and solo scenes, lost myself in interesting and complicated dance details which according to the music seemed right, in fact necessary, to me. But the more I got involved in this musical work, the more uncomfortable I began to feel — until I began to realize: the simpler the better. Could I have said more than Stravinsky had already expressed in his grandiose music? Certainly not! Then I would have to leave the lead to the music and subordinate the dance creation to it. This, of course, meant to relinquish completely all attempts at painting and illustrating the subtleties and colorful shadings of the music through the dance. But the work as a whole benefited by it. Because in its final simplified conception as a large choric dance, the dance became coordinated to the musical work as the moving spatial form in which it could also live and endure as "scenic event."

## The Dance Fulfilling its Task as Applied Art

Opera, operetta, the musical, and drama use the dance as incidental event, as an element creating an atmosphere, or to loosen up the scenic action and to serve as adornment.

Only in rare cases — as in Gluck's operas, which broke with past tradition — is the dance visualized as an organic part of the musical plot from the very beginning. Having sold my soul to the dance, I deemed it important to let it have a place beyond its usual dancing "interlude" in the musical theatre! Of course, one cannot generalize. But the stage works of Gluck, Händel, and a few other composers who lean toward the scenic oratorio rather than the grand opera, leave sufficient room for a meaningful elaboration of their scenes through the medium of the dance.

And so I made the attempt — with extraordinary stage effect — to banish the singing chorus from the stage to the orchestra pit; in its place I put the dancing chorus. Its task: to shape the space and to create an atmosphere. Its message: to give life to action or to contemplation. The singing actors left on stage thus received a dramatically or lyrically moving background against which they stood out the stronger because, as individually profiled personalities, they created a consciously achieved, effective contrast to the rhythmically bound and sharply stylized character of the expressive chorus.

In the last act of Gluck's opera *Alcestis* the dominion of death was built up only with means that were of the dance. It was an infinitely sombre and, at the same time, threatening space which received its architectural structure through the frozen figures of the dancers standing there like shapes of grey stone, and which achieved rhythmic life through groups of figures moving shadowlike, passing through this space and swathing it with veils of mist. Its special effectiveness, only coming about through the use of dance, was imbedded in the unreality of its metamorphosis, in the almost deadly loneliness of a lost or forgotten landscape which inexorably kept itself apart from any range of human reality.

Called and admonished by this vision-shaped space, Alcestis crosses the threshold separating her forever from the realm of life. Admitted to his dominion by the god of the dead, guided by him and protected on all sides by the milling shades, she is led step by step and as though in a growing transparency of her corporeality toward her destiny: toward the extinction of her own life, which she voluntarily sacrifices in order to preserve the life of another human being, the one man loved without limits.

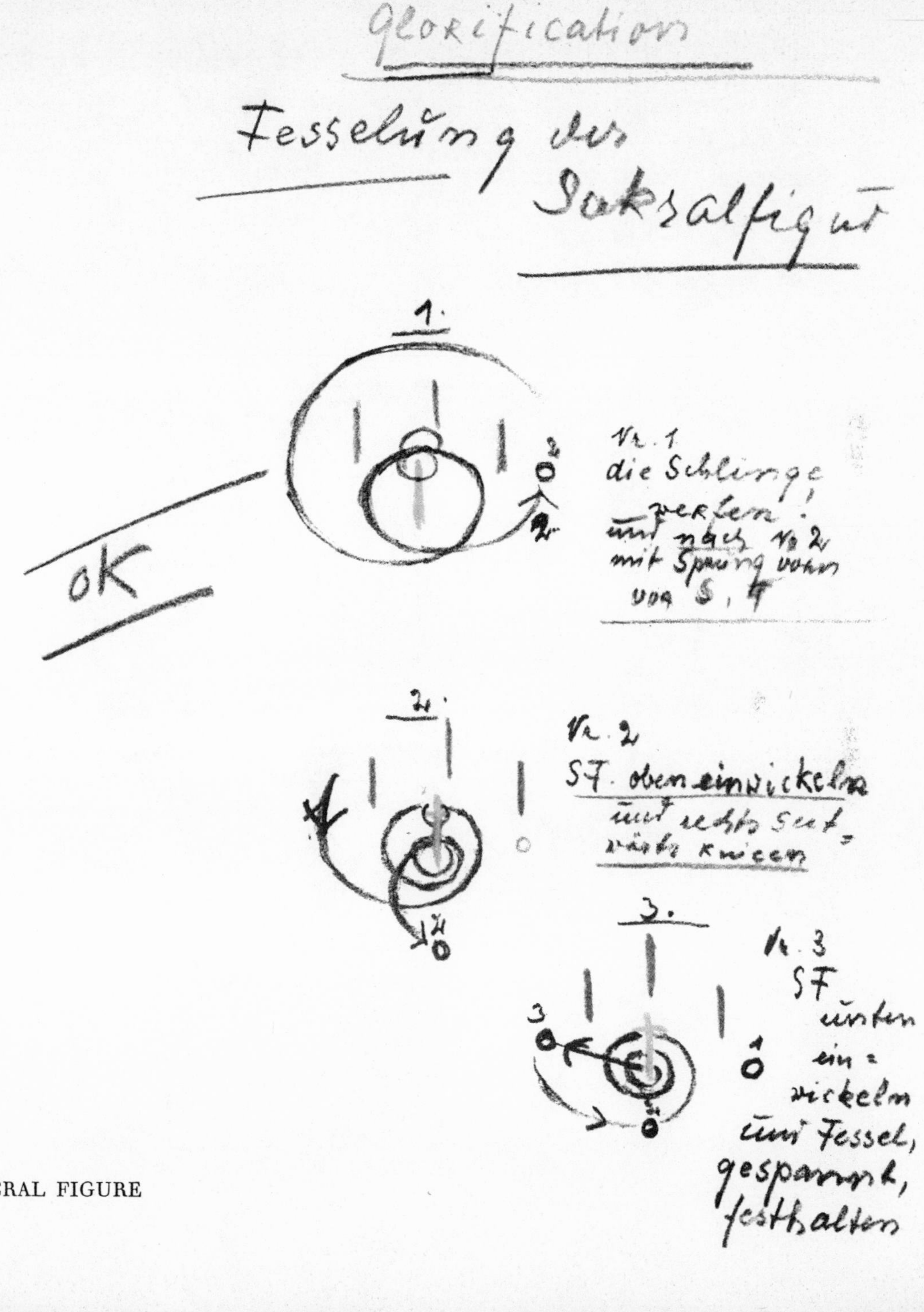

Glorification

Fesselung der Sakralfigur

1.

ok

Nr. 1
die Schlinge
perlen!
und nach Nr. 2
mit Sprung vorn
von S. 4

2.

Nr. 2
SF. oben einwickeln
und rechts seit,
rücks knieen

3.

Nr. 3
SF
unten
ein=
wickeln
und Fessel,
gespannt,
festhalten

THE RITES OF SPRING    THE SHACKLING OF THE SACRAL FIGURE

Chaconne

grosser Kreis,
von dem aus es in
den Schluss geleitet
werden könnte. —

Liebesschaukel
motiv 2

4

hübsch —
aber nicht
genug Tänzer
Paare

dafür —

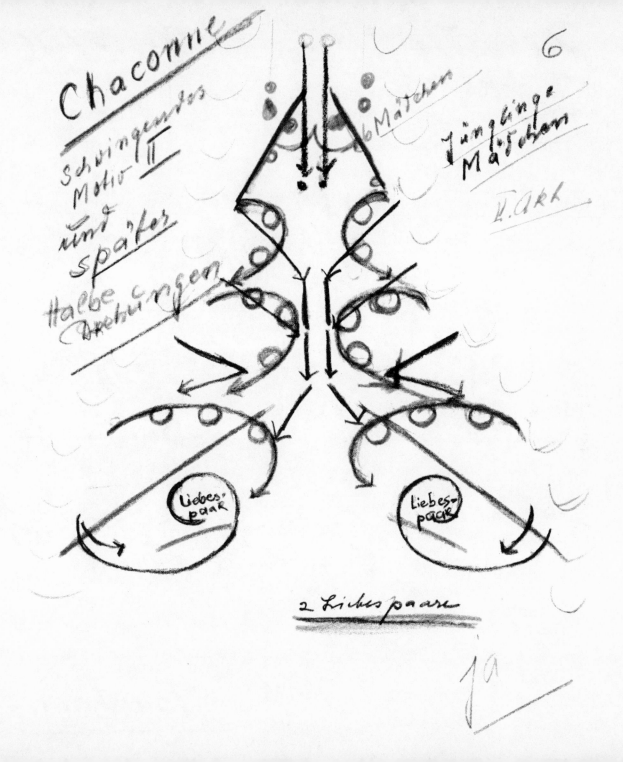

SKETCHES FOR ALCESTIS

Alkestis
II AKT

Ouverture

Der Todeshain.

ALCESTIS
IN THE DOMINION OF DEATH

GLUCK    ORPHEUS AND EURYDICE

DANCE OF THE FURIES

# Ceremonial Figure

I brought home from a Balkan tour a song which had been given to me by a Hungarian musician after a dance performance in Budapest. A crystal clear and capricious tunefulness that was dancing throughout and asking to be choreographed.

And as so often when something preoccupied my mind and wanted to be expressed, I shut myself in my golden room, leaned my head against the softly singing Siamese gong, and listened to myself deep within. I did so until a pose emerged out of this musing and resolved itself into the stylistically corresponding gesture and, with it, into the first careful step which released the now awakened body and surrendered it to space. However insignificant the discovered motif was, it stood its ground. I started to work. But it needed many detours before the "ceremonial figure" emerged from the basic motif and its movement development. Thus, it disturbed me that the feet could move too freely, and I was searching for a possibility to hamper them in moving forward and to provide them with the visibly limited space which they demanded. A few atttempts misfired. But then I had the idea of taking one of those colored hoops used by children playing in the street. I sewed it into the hem of my wide rehearsal skirt. And lo and behold: it formed a bell-like shape, and within its limited compass the movement found its own master. Every little step caused the bell to swing. And it was right. But every kind of intensified step made it swing too wide. And that should not happen.

It was self-evident that the rhythm of the feet had to fit the moving bell-like shape and, in its crescendo becoming more and more pointed, poise and gesture had to match it. The ceremonial character emerged in ever clearer form and surrendered to an uncompromisingly unified style in which I was no longer the shaping force but merely the executing organ.

What restraint it put upon myself! What torture to have to force one's expressive powers — coming to the fore time and again — into an absolute form which took on its own independence! The restraint was not yet sufficient. Because there still was the human face, which in spite of its disciplined immobility bore the features of Mary Wigman and did not want to subordinate itself to the natural rules of the "ceremonial figure."

What was to be done? The only way out, the only possible banishment, was and became: the mask. I asked the help of a young mask-maker who, in the circle of my students, experimented with Japanese No masks. Daily he sat in the corner of my studio and observed the growing of the choreographed figure. He — so to speak — projected himself into this figure. Then he disappeared in the forests of Moritzburg to look for the wood best suited for the carving. The mask he brought was an almost demonic translation of my face. I fell in love with it at first sight. But when I put it on my face, I had a very peculiar feeling. Instead of having a soothing effect, it was upsetting. It underscored the personal where it should have depersonalized.

Again my mask-maker vanished and left me to my apprehension. How would the second version turn out? But then, when he put it carefully into my hands, my enthusiasm knew no limits. Here it was, the face for which the "ceremonial figure" longed! The finely grained wood was carved down to a chinalike thinness, transfixed into an oblong shape, with a mere suggestion of human features. Mouth and eyebrows painted with greyish blue brush strokes on the ivory-colored wood. Two small slits for the eyes. Nothing else! But even in this abstraction was retained a trace of the personal dance face.

To wear the mask was torture. Like a flat bowl, like a second skin, it rested on the face; and its carved features, caught in the wood, marked my own face. When I took it off after the dance, I could not help feeling that the mask had identified itself with me — or I with the mask — to such an extent that I was gripped by the fear that I would never be able to get rid of my mask-face. In order to be able to breathe at all, time and again I had to take the mask off while working on the dance. Otherwise I would have suffocated. Its only orifice, its only supply of air, consisted of the two narrow slits for the eyes, which permitted no vision and barely let me recognize whether I moved in light or darkness. In order not to endanger myself on stage, I was compelled to move within a tightly measured space with an exactitude marked to each centimeter. Torture in every respect!

But what bliss, what triumph that one had done it after all and that the slightly exotic dance-figure — now become more exalted, noble, unapproachably beckoning from afar — could assert itself on the stage!

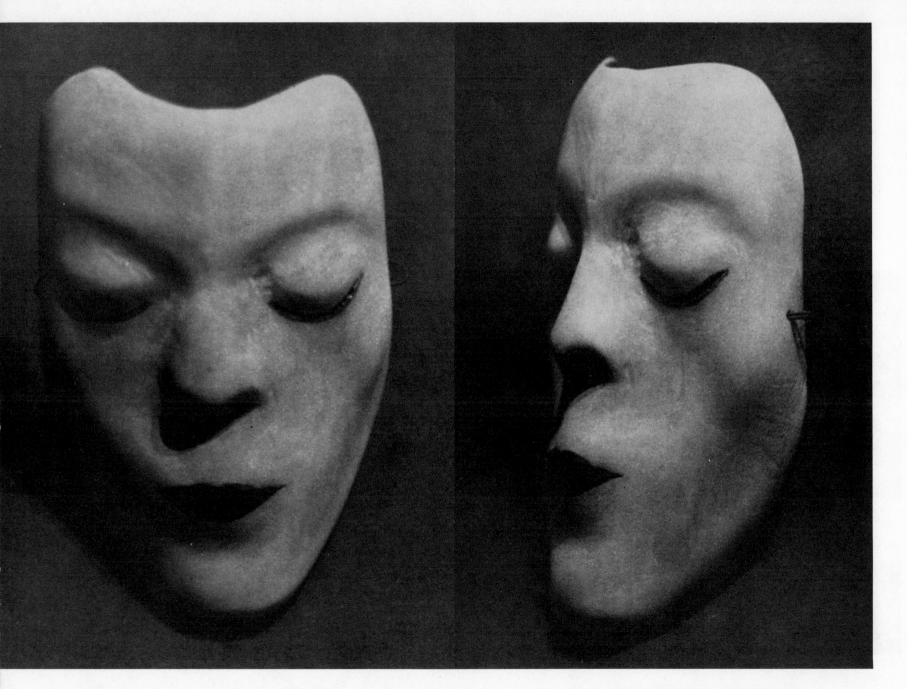

CEREMONIAL FIGURE   THE MASK

MONOTONY (WHIRL DANCE)

# Monotony (Whirl Dance)

The Chinese gong was placed in a room of its own, from the center of which it governed everything else. It was shaped like a fat-bellied bronze pail which did not look as if it possessed magic powers. To have it yield its secret, one had to know the magic formula which alone could make it sound.

Actually, there was magic in the tone-evoking, infinitely careful gesture of the human hand, which had to move with the greatest sureness. The tone was not produced by hitting the gong with a clapper, but by a slow and constantly circling movement of a leather-covered stick stroking the inside of the highly polished edge. This is what is done with wineglasses when one wants to make them sound. And just as the glass emits its tone only when it vibrates as a whole, so it took a while until the deep droning sound of the gong began to leave its metallic shell. The whole room seemed to wait in a peculiar state of tension for the growing of this sound. I too waited for it, ready with all my senses, as if I expected an apparition to manifest itself at any moment. But then the unexpected happened! It was not the bronze body of the gong which began to sound, but the whole room that vibrated. It was as if the earth had opened up and embraced everything with its warm breath. From everywhere, from all directions, a bewitching whispering and humming came toward me. The air seemed to shimmer, opalescent lights were dancing up and down, and one wave of warmth after another began to fill the room.

I felt as if I were witnessing an hour of birth. Now, from the whispering and murmuring, from shimmer and glimmer, the sound-turned-tone emerged in all its purity. In immaculate beauty it went its course, finding completion in unending rotation. Full, warm, and dark, it was the voice of the depth, playfully alive in all its shadings. With breath-taking urgency it grew to its full strength, bronze that sounded and sang, in whose embrace the beating of one's own blood seemed to determine the rhythm of its vibrating revolutions. The walls turned around, the ceiling turned around, and so did the floor. Which was sound, which space, which movement? And who knew the magic formula commanding it to stand still? From where would come the deliverance from this condition which was pain and bliss at one and the same time?

The tone itself had been victorious. Then, with imperial calm, suddenly it seemed to be still; and, as if under the force of a majestic command, the natural order of things was restored. One found the way back to oneself, again one could breathe, feel, see, and one was witness to a touching farewell.

Just as this sound had appeared, it vanished again. And perhaps this was the most beautiful thing: to experience how the earth-born tone went back through the secret door from which it had emerged, how it returned to the womb of the earth which protectively closed around it. What it left behind was the tenderness and sweetness of a silence complete in itself. One wanted to lie down in it, to sleep and to dream.

I know that this experience remained with me for a long time and that I must be grateful to it for many things. But I only became conscious of this much later. *Monotony,* a solo dance from the group work *Celebration,* came about because of this "tone experience" given to me as a present by the Chinese gong. Only long after the genesis of this dance did I become aware of how deeply it was rooted in that experience. *Monotony* accompanied me through many stages of my artistic development from 1927 to 1942 and became, so to speak, the ancestor of all whirl dances later created by other dancers. I have never felt the need to change it or to give it up in order to leave it to the past. I was so sure of it that, torn out of the deepest sleep, I could have danced it without mistake and without having to think of the sequence of its complicated dance forms for a single moment.

In spite of this I was terrified by it! And when I prepared for the dance in those seconds between stepping onstage and hearing the familiar sound of the curtain going up, every time I was overcome by a tremor which I had difficulty in calming down.

Did the reason for this fear lie in the realization that I would again surrender to dying one of those peculiarly unreal deaths which a work of art created by the dancing body demands of its performer?

It was as if I had to set out on a dangerous road, a road whose destination was unknown to me, a destination from which I might never find my way back. But after the first solemn bow, after the first hesitating steps, the feeling of quiet came back to me, and with it the feeling of inescapability which, in its own logic, meant deliverance from the burden of the all-too-personal.

The musical form of this dance was the simplest conceivable. It limited itself to the mere accompaniment of the danced sequences. Piano and drum: in constant repetition a short, Oriental-like motif characterized by two shifting accents. And with it, the exciting uninterrupted taps, raps, and the urgency of the muted drumbeats, monotonous, insistent, only changing pace and volume according to the dance rhythm. Beneath the wide-paced steps and above the rhythmically turning gestures of the arms, there was the big circle of space spanned like an arc, narrowing itself in a spiral and contracting to one point which was called the center, which became the center and remained the center. Nothing more happened, only the relentless turning around one's own axis.

Fixed to the same spot and spinning in the monotony of the whirling movement, one lost oneself gradually in it until the turns seemed to detach themselves from the body, and the world around it started to turn. Not turning oneself, but being turned, being the center, being the quiet pole in the vortex of rotation!

Arch and dome, no sky above me — no direction, no goal — circling and turning in a spiral-like movement up and down, without beginning, without end — a tender rocking, with the arms reaching out, painful and blissful again in a crescendo of self-destructive lust, surging and ebbing, flowing back higher and faster, ever faster — the vortex seized me, the waters rose. The vortex dragged me down. Ever higher, ever faster, hunted, whipped, rushed. Will it never end? Why does no one speak the redeeming word, stopping this madness? With a last desperate exertion, control over one's willpower is found again.

A jerk pierces the body, compelling it to stand still at the moment of the fastest turn; now the body is stretched high, lifted on tiptoe, with the arms thrown up, grasping a non-existent support. A breathless pause, an eternity long, lasting, however, only a few seconds. And then the sudden letting go, the fall of the relaxed body into the depth with only one sensation still alive: that of a complete incorporeal state. And in that state only one wish: never be forced to get up again, to be allowed to lie there just like this, through all eternity.

But after a short moment of quiet there were people, there was an audience applauding. I had learned to discipline myself. Whether the auditorium turned around me, whether my head droned or my heart was beating like mad and my breath came in gasps — the minute the curtain went up again, I had to and wanted to be there again to take my bows. Once more it had turned out well. Once more I had got away by the skin of my teeth.

# Witch Dance

While cleaning a closet in my school, I found an old worn piece of brocade. It had served generations of my students for costume studies, and it showed all the traces of its final disintegration. I was at the point of destroying it when I suddenly remembered what this fabric once was: the costume for the *Witch Dance*, which belonged to one of the "great" solo dances of my career. I saw myself standing in a Swiss silk store and staring in fascination at this splendor spread out before me: bold designs in metal threads on a copper-red background shimmering in gold and silver traced in black — exciting, wild, barbaric. I was as if hypnotized and bought the fabric against my better judgment. It was outrageously expensive, and I knew only too well that I had no use for it. I had a bad conscience, and thus this piece of splendor went into the fabric drawer of my costume closet where it remained hidden from my eyes for years. I created new solo and group dances, the various characters of *Visions* grew into being. The creative urge got hold of me again. What its intention was, where it would lead me, was not yet clearly recognizable. Only the restlessness was there, and some kind of evil greed I felt in my hands, which pressed themselves clawlike into the ground as if they had wanted to take root. I had the sensation of being full to the point of bursting and near desperation. I felt it ought to be possible to give shape to whatever it was that distressed me beyond measure.

Sometimes at night I slipped into the studio and worked myself up into a rhythmic intoxication in order to come closer to the slowly stirring character. I could feel how everything pointed toward a clearly defined dance figure. The richness of rhythmic ideas was overwhelming. But something was opposed to their becoming lucid and orderly, something that forced the body time and again into a sitting or squatting position in which the greedy hands could take possession of the ground.

When, one night, I returned to my room utterly agitated, I looked into the mirror by chance. What it reflected was the image of one possessed, wild and dissolute, repelling and fascinating. The hair unkempt, the eyes deep in their sockets, the nightgown shifted about, which made the body appear almost shapeless: there she was — the witch — the earth-bound creature with her unrestrained, naked instincts, with her insatiable lust for life, beast and woman at one and the same time.

I shuddered at my own image, at the exposure of this facet of my ego which I had never allowed to emerge in such unashamed nakedness. But, after all, isn't a bit of a witch hidden in every hundred-per-cent female, no matter which form its origin may have?

All that had to be done was to tame this elemental creature, to mold her and to work on one's own body as on a sculpture. It was wonderful to abandon oneself to the craving for evil, to imbibe the powers which usually dared to stir only weakly beneath one's civilized surface. But all this had to be surrendered to the rules of creation, the rules which had to be based on the essence and character of the dance-shape itself to define and reflect it truly once and for all. I had to take this into consideration and to be extremely careful so that the original creative urge was neither weakened nor blocked in the process of molding and shaping.

Does not the power, the magnificence of all creative art lie in knowing how to force chaos into form? A form which as an idea, as symbol, and as simile becomes, so to speak, second nature to prove itself as a work of art on a higher level? The artistic form is not an end in itself, is not being created to turn numb and torpid the fermenting matter from which it arises. It is the receptacle which, time and again, grows hot with, and is inflamed by, the living content until the mutual melting-down process is fully completed, and from this point on only the artistic action speaks to us. My witch figure also had to be brought to the point of this entity and had to receive her profile in an outward and plastic manifestation which was hers. The scales fell from my eyes: the piece of brocade! Did it not possess, in its barbaric beauty, in its splendiferous ruthlessness, something that corresponded to the revolting character of the dance? And there was still left the first and never used mask of the *Ceremonial Figure*, whose features were my own translated into the demonic. I suddenly knew that fabric and mask belonged together and that they had had to wait this long for their return from exile in order that, as costume and mask, they might give the *Witch Dance* its representative, its very own stage image. The creation of the dance went faster than I had imagined. The discovered motifs fell into place in an unbroken chain and stood up to the demands of the composition. Only the mask caused some headache. In contrast to the mask in the *Ceremonial Figure*, which preserved its immaculate expressive smoothness through all phases of the dance, also in contrast to the frighteningly masked figures of the

*Dance of Death* which was later created as a group dance, the *Witch Dance* mask possessed its own personal life. Every movement of the body evoked a changed expression of the face; depending on the position of the head, the eyes seemed to close or to open. As a matter of fact, even around the mouth — intimated with a few strokes of the brush — there seemed to play a smile which, in its unfathomableness, was reminiscent of the Sphinx. The body, too, burdened with heaviness, possessed something of the lurking, animal-like quality in the image of the enigmatic Sphinx, even though only by way of intimation.

"Keep the secret . . ." What a discovery! By incorporating this element, which became clarified through the warning gesture covering the mouth, through the play of question and answer between a remote background plunged into twilight and the glaring foreground action, the character of the dance, tumultuous in itself, found its corresponding opposite pole, for which I had searched in vain for a long time. Only now *Witch Dance* was really accomplished.

I believe that *Witch Dance* was the only one among my solo dances which did not make me shake with stage fright before every performance. How I loved it, this growing into the excitement of its expressive world, how intensely I tried in each performance to feel myself back into the original creative condition of *Witch Dance* and to fulfill its stirring form by returning to the very point where it all began!

WITCH DANCE

WITCH DANCE

SHIFTING LANDSCAPE

INVOCATION

# Shifting Landscape

The sky was cloudy. There had been many a storm, and the outspread wings in their soaring flight apparently wanted to lose some of their elasticity.

What had struck me hardest was the necessity to dissolve my first dance group, whose members, without exception, had gone through my school. In five years of work I had formed them into an instrument, a harmonious body, which had become exemplary in every respect. We had worked out many different programs together (the last and most beautiful one was *Celebration*) and were wonderfully attuned to each other. We had gone on many tours, we had experienced good and bad days together. And wherever we appeared, at home or abroad, we prepared and conquered the ground for the "new German dance."

Now they were scattered to the four winds, my faithful ones, and with them had gone my accompanist of many years. It was a difficult parting which, at the same time, was also the termination of my first ten years of independent artistic work. And more than once I felt like losing heart, dreading the toil of starting from scratch again.

But then the clouds seemed to disperse once more. The new generation started to prove itself, I could dare to set to work on the first big choric task of my life, the choreography of the dramatically charged dance sequences of the *Totenmal,* a work by Albert Talhoff, the performance of which took place a year later (1930) in Munich. I had signed the contract for my first long American tour.

Through official and private channels I was assured of a rather large sum of money which made it possible to form a new dance group. We had just finished a very successful "international" summer course in Dresden, and the advanced students of my school had graduated without exception. Now I could take my vacation in a lighthearted and carefree mood. I made the trip to the south of France in a friend's car. The sun was shining, the world was wide and life was beautiful! Even the feeling of sweet melancholy caused by an impending leave-taking — which accompanies any beautiful experience — did not spell gloom for me. It rather added to the enhancement of the joy of life. And every new day seemed to confirm this feeling. The landscape flitted by: flat stretches with the bright band of the retreating road before the eyes, a gradual climb and steep slopes, gently winding river valleys, spread-out lakes circled by chains of mountains, the Bay of Biscay; the Pyrenees; the fertile garden of France; Provence — Carcassonne, Lourdes, Marseilles — the coast of the Mediterranean.

Everything was constantly changing, but never restless, never hurried. Aloneness was as wonderful as being together was harmonious. I was very happy. Because it was the time of promise and blossoming — also of my blossoming.

*Shifting Landscape* was the cycle of solo dances which were the immediate result of this summer trip. Image and form combined themselves without any lengthy roundabout way and received the right shape in quick succession. The dances grew into a colorful flower bouquet which caught and contained the glow of sun-happy summer days, the secret of star-studded nights, and the wistful sweetness of overcast and rainy hours.

## Invocation

There I stood, erect and tense, throwing out the first sweeping gesture. Arms and legs swung through space in equal arcs, in equal rhythms, and became the defining motif for an invocation which, in spite of its moderate restraint, was heroic in character. It was the same emotion I felt when, for the first time after the war — the First World War! — I set foot on French soil. There was so much sympathy and adoration in all that France meant to me, French culture and French *esprit*. But also my own roots in everything Germanic, and my adherence to it, were in this feeling. It was like a meeting, it was an invocation that went across and a being called that came from over there.

Now the inexpressible, the indefinable wanted to become dance and found its visual expression in the danced form which as *Invocation* was the first dance of the cycle, *Shifting Landscape*.

For the second dance, the *Seraphic Song*, the Cathedral of Strassburg and the Isenheim Altar in Colmar acted as godparents.

## Face of Night

But when I felt compelled to create the third dance of this cycle, I did not immediately know that war would play its part in it again; and that this time it would be gloomy, terrifying, ghostlike, and very lonesome. The dance was already broadly sketched and almost completed in its essential features when I suddenly became aware that the fundamental idea on which it was built had the shape of a vertical cross.

And I saw again the shattering image of the German Soldiers' Cemetery in the Vosges mountains: cross after cross, a whole slope of the mountain filled with black crosses — the names on them almost obliterated by the weather. And farther up, the nameless crosses, the graves of the masses — *"Cimetière de guerre des soldats allemands"* — bordered by a few field stones. Nothing else. No human figure in mourning who would have bent down with grief, not even a faded flower to bear witness to a loving hand. No trees, no bushes, not a blade of grass! Even nature seemed to have retreated from this place of inviolable silence and limitless forlornness.

The terrifying finality of death — here it was, naked and without mercy. Commanded to die, lined up to die, mowed down and crushed by the indiscriminate grip of the mechanically working war machine — even the last place of rest organized, and now lying there as if a long, long time ago a cataclysmic event of nature had taken place. And yet it was the work of man.

The sun stood hot and high in the summer sky, but I shivered as if I were in an underground cave.

Only a few turns down the steep road, and we stood in front of the French Soldiers' Cemetery. The same picture, only by far more conciliatory. The crosses were white, surrounded by a protective wall; a chapel was erected from where the litany of prayers reached the ear. There were people, single and in groups, accompanied by priests; and flowers, lovingly planted and cared for next to the graves. And yet this picture could not make one forget the feeling of horror evoked by the forgotten cemetery of the German soldiers.

Now I knew why *Face of Night* could only emerge from the rigid image of the cross. And now I knew also where the concept had come from in which the dance themes — varied and executed with their fundamental ideas intact — were brought to their final completion. No one had to know about the experience which was behind it, and probably no one did know. But the message of the dance became clear through the acclaim of the public. It was a loud *J'accuse* which bespoke the ghastly terror of ultimate aloneness.

FACE OF NIGHT

PASTORAL

# Pastoral

I was lying on the beach, lost in a feeling of relaxation, doing nothing, thinking of nothing, beholden to nothing, completely abandoned to the moment. The sky above was blue.

But again and again the thunder of the waves broke into the sleep-happy monotony. Far out the waves tested their strength against the chalky rocks covered with shells and sent their foam in silvery fountains high up into the shimmering air. To be carried high up, to throw oneself into the glittering surf, to surrender oneself again, refreshed and cooled, to the delicious passivity of the sun-swept beach!

The slightly raised arm swung to and fro in the air without resistance, the fingers moved playfully in the rhythm of wave and tide. Everything was so soft and warm, so pleasantly weightless, everything had the freshness of a dawning day about it.

A little melody came back to me. I had heard it played on a shepherd's flute high on a plateau in the Pyrenees. It remained with me and came back to me when I began to choreograph the *Pastoral*. As a matter of fact, it became the leit-motif of the dance. A European flute, a Chinese gong, an Indian double bell, an African and an Indian drum — these were the instruments which, in harmonious unison, accompanied and supported the melodic-rhythmic structure of the dance.

The light blue costume was studded with large, wavelike silver ornaments, the skirt lined with a glowing red. It was very wide and spread about the relaxed figure lying on the floor like the valve of a shimmering shell. It clung to the body. It rippled with the fast rhythmic movements of the feet and surged about the swinging wide gestures. It was like laughter when the red mingled with the blue on which the silver glittered. This dance had a definitely lyrical character. Its melodic line received a soft rhythmic underscoring in even intervals.

Gently rocking, the body gradually rose from its resting position and freed the feet so that they might play in the sand. They enjoyed it and outdid themselves in small and fast turns in a challenging interplay, gliding past each other like the delicate foamy crests of receding waves. The steps grew wider and raised the dancing body in the momentum of its big turns, opening up in space and slowly ebbing into the blissful calm of the original, passive feeling of being rocked, until this too died away in a last soft fading gesture of the hand — and the dance had come to an end.

# Festive Rhythm

What is there to tell about *Festive Rhythm*, the fifth dance of the cycle? To me, it meant the essence of a summer holiday and the experience of a bullfight at Pamplona.

A festive day for men! Because there was hardly a Spanish woman and only a few female tourists to be seen in the surging crowd at the open market or in the press of spectators on the seats of the arena. The excitement mounted almost unbearably. But I noticed how, the closer we came to the hour of the fight, the more well-behaved were the people in a manner I have never observed before at such popular entertainments.

Mixed into the hum of human voices was the penetrating twang of guitars and mandolins. A throaty song rose over it, then was drowned out by the blaring fanfares of the brass band — an ear-splitting noise which, nevertheless, was not chaotic, but had an elementary, unified rhythm. The shirts and neckerchiefs of the young men shone in all colors: red, yellow, orange, blue. They were gathered in big bunches, or swam like gay islands above and between the black worn by the older men. And all this: the colored bunches and swimming islands, the colorful and the dark in motion — up and down, up and down — in one passionately excited and exciting vibrato.

I too was gripped by this expectant excitement. The eye could hardly absorb all these images. To sit still in the midst of all this swarming and swirling agitation became tormenting. Beneath me the circle of the arena was spread out, bare and empty, and yet it was a part of all this tension which was nearing the boiling point.

Then it started, a little operatic at first, with much feeling for display — and a great deal of self-confident carriage in the contestants who presented themselves in the traditional costume of their calling. The noise had died down somewhat and for a moment ceased entirely as thousands of eyes, in feverish expectation, turned to that one gate which was now opened. The bull entered the scene.

What was a game to the Spanish spectators — a game whose rules everyone knew, a game which animated, intoxicated, and inspired them — threw me into panic: the confrontation between man and animal. No, not man against animal and not animal against man — but creature against creature, peers of each other in a game which was a struggle of life and death.

The shadow of the great god Pan emerged and from then on hovered above the events which he determined. Ur-power and the demon of earth-bound instincts of many thousand years were on one side. The feet beating the ground — the malevolently lowered head with the dangerous curve of its powerful horns — the thick-set body — the black and brown hide glistening with sweat in the sun — and the red ribbon of blood which, as if fed from a gushing spring, covered the back of the animal and left its traces in the sand. The legs wide apart, a position in which mighty power renewed itself time and again — the revengeful fury with which the hunted animal was ready to attack again and again, its flanks shaking and shivering when, cunningly and threateningly, it set out for a new deadly thrust, knowing instinctively only one thing, wanting only one thing: the annihilation of its adversary. And on the opposite side, the man — the torero who, with intellectual superiority, had gained his means of fighting from rigid training and body control. With the taut elegance of his posture, the elastic leaps, the almost flirtatious turns and gyrations as he parried the attack, he became the ideal of the male dancer, lifting the gory fight to the level of play, arrogant in his challenge, subtle and evasive like a lizard, and ravishing in breathtaking moments of sudden standstill in which he faced the rage-blinded assault of his enemy.

The yelling and shouting of the crowd — inciting or insulting, contemptuous or approving — did not differentiate between the two fighting partners. I was afraid for the life of the man, but just as much did I worry about the life of the animal, which up to its last breath defended itself with every weapon provided it by nature.

All this was a spectacle no longer — and it touched one facet of my being of which, until then, I had not been conscious. Once there were Indian tribes who elected the bull, the buffalo, as primary ruler of the prairie and as ancestor of their tribe. I suddenly understood all this, and the great god Pan smiled. . . . Then it was over, and we drove into the gradually darkening night, which cooled our burning temples and also slowly quieted down the tempest in our blood.

I immediately knew that I would retain and create the experience of this day as a dance. I wanted to take up fencing, wanted to take lessons in Spanish dancing. But the experience neither turned into a bull-fight nor a "Spanish dance." It became *Festive Rhythm*, in which the sun-drenched landscape danced along, to which the exciting atmosphere of the arena contributed its share — and perhaps there was added to it a drop of the aroma that gave this day its peculiarly Spanish note.

I had to work very hard to find the right form for this dance; because this tight theme did not lend itself to any epic breadth. Not even the ending of a gesture fading out in silence was right for it. Crystal clear was the dance in the contours of its positions, brilliantly rhythmic in its metrical structure, sophisticated and exacting in the lightninglike changes of the use of space; radiating victory and still in the smallest detail vibrating with excitement, with the whirl of colors and shapes and the merciless heat of a shadeless midsummer sun.

The feet planted powerfully against the floor, jerking up in staccato rhythm, or, under the arched span, thrusting forward like the point of a sharp dagger. The legs in a bent position or stretched to the utmost ecstatic tension widening the torso.

The arms in short, angular gestures sharply bent, or motionless, tautly stretched out horizontally. They punctuated the rhythm of legs and arms, seemed to stand up in a gesture of defiance or incitement. Horizontal against vertical. Dimension against dimension. Yet not a struggle at all. And least of all the imitation of a bullfight. Rather it changed into an homage, a paean sung to the fervidly experienced festive day.

As strenuous — and strenuous to exhaustion! — as this dance was during its genesis and execution, it was wonderful to dance in the sequence of the program. Because like a great challenge, like a clarion call, it stood between the lyrical *Pastoral* and the Capriccio of the *Dance of Summer* immediately following it in its creative concept as well as in the program.

Actually, it finished the cycle. But enough of this. The exuberance was yet too great. And thus the three *Gipsy Dances* came into being — put like an exclamation mark at the end. The expression of joy of life per se, abounding in strength, technically brilliant and ever changing between sorrow and bliss, between gaiety and melancholy, elating and catching in their effect.

It was wonderful to be able to dance, to know how to dance — yes — and wonderful to make other people also enthusiastic for the dance. None of my other solo programs was performed as often as *Shifting Landscape*. I danced it in Berlin, Vienna, and Zürich, in London, Paris, and New York. It did not have the dramatic impact of the ensuing cycle, *Sacrifice*, nor the resigned wisdom of the later-created *Autumnal Dances*. But it showed a brimming abundance, a fully flowing and glowing power, probably given to man only once in his life, at a time when, like the midsummer sun, he stands at the zenith of his creative power, in the summer of his own life. . . .

FESTIVE RHYTHM

DANCE OF SUMMER

# Dance of Summer

*Dance of Summer* was my personal favorite and, strangely enough, it also became the favorite of the American public, which asked for it time and again.

"Who is the lucky one?" somebody had once asked me after a rehearsal. Well, it was a love song, and there was much tender playfulness in the enticing promise, in the denying oneself and in the yielding. But was it really dedicated to one person alone? Wasn't it also meant, in an even deeper sense, for the summer whose wind brought me the song and to which it was returned in clandestine greeting — as a gift of gratitude?

There was so much warmth in it — fulfillment as well as a first presentiment of changes destined to come. And a bit of self-ridicule was also thrown into it. From time to time a little mocking smile flitted through the gestures as if they wanted to say: Don't take us too seriously, we won't last, we are only one of the many reflections in the mirror of your life and are only glowing as long as the summer sun hits us.

How I loved the costume of this dance, its silken velvet clinging so tenderly to me — golden yellow like a ripening wheat field atop the finely woven silver brocade which rustled faintly when touched by the warmth of the body, and with each movement, seemed to fade like the summer sun when it exchanges its golden light with the glistening silver of noon.

The dance was a tango, whose features, however, were so far reduced that its remaining effect was a finely organized rhythmic vibration; and, as if touched by a soft summer's breeze, the dance had a transparency in everything physical through which eroticism fluttered like a butterfly.

It whispered in secret and threw small capers of hand gestures into the air like barely audible words of love. It was like a poppy on a swaying stem, and in its crescendi it was like a concert of shrilling cicadas when, at high noon, they drown out all other sounds of nature. It was like noon when the still air in the heat of summer starts to dance without any other purpose than to surrender to a feeling of happiness which appears to be without end and yet lasts a moment only.

# Storm Song

The feet race across the floor, chasing the body in wide curves through space, as though whipped by the winds, driven by the storm. Blindly, the body throws itself into mercilessly hammering rhythms. Seeking protection, it crouches, is being tossed about and bent — back and forth, back and forth — rearing up and falling like a tree hit by lightning. The body remains breathless in the short pauses of calm, only to expose itself to the raging wind again, gripped and shaken by it, driven ahead and turned about on its own axis — until left exhausted and thrown to the ground in dull indifference by a last gust.

The costume: a tremendously bright red chiffon mantle, obliterating the body outlines to a point of un-recognizability. The face, too, utterly depersonalized under the red veil mask.

Above the swinging gestures of the arms, the light fabric swelled and was blown up and turned into cloudy images, stirring and drifting away only to tumble down like a torrent, rippling and slowly becoming smooth; then, during short moments of rest, the dancing body again received its human proportions and shivered under the onslaught of the storm. The kettledrums rumbled, the drums throbbed, hammered, rattled, and raged.

A furioso, a bacchanal, a lustful scream of the creature abandoning herself to the unleashed elements — experienced high up on the mountain pass in ecstasy — and now newly inflamed and turned in the creative process into an allegoric image: a single red flaming beacon: the storm song.

DANCE OF SUMMER

STORM SONG

SERAPHIC SONG

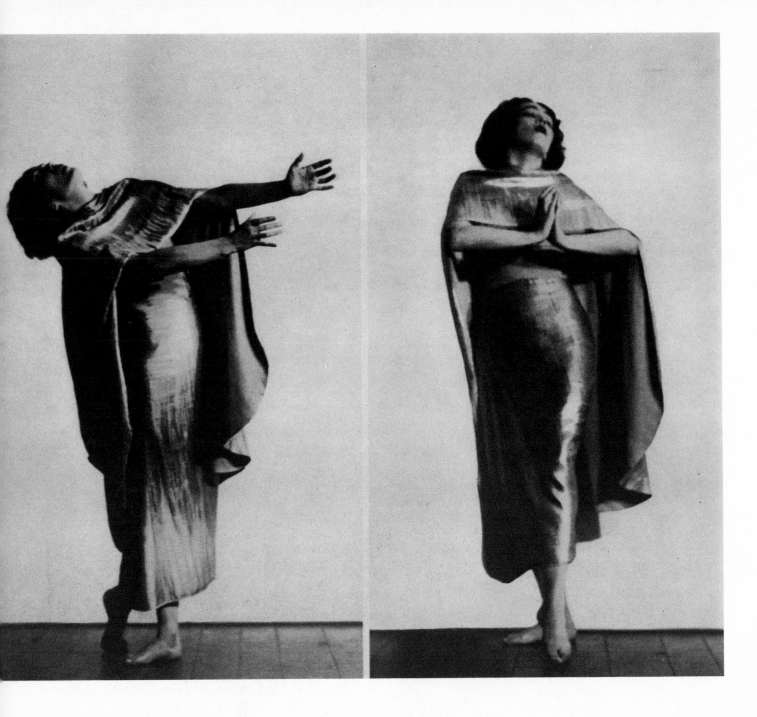

SERAPHIC SONG

# Seraphic Song

Two musical experiences, each in its own way, led to dance creations. Two instruments, significant of two worlds of sound: a European glass piano and a Chinese bowl gong. Europe and Asia. Music of the spheres and earthborn music. When, for the first time, I heard this music, I thought I witnessed the birth of music. Not the birth of music as shape and form, but its reason for being, its origin and, so to speak, its primal tone. In this wood-paneled room, specifically built to house the glass piano, was a peculiarly acoustic atmosphere. It apparently desired to be nothing else but an extended and intensified sounding board. As the musician's hands lifted the cover of the instrument with almost gentle cautiousness, I was enchanted by the beauty of the glass bells, with the delicate colorfulness of their paint and the grace of their rhythmic arrangement.

But I was not prepared at all for the enchantment that overwhelmed me when I heard the very first sound. Something happened that I had physically experienced up to then only when dancing, when, ecstatic and completely abandoned to the airy sphere, one loses the feeling of gravity and seems to float. The voice of the glass bells was not of this world. It was the voice of the seraph, the light-flooded angel, who, with silver trumpet at his lips, soars up and vanishes into the ether. And thus, in soaring upward and losing all boundaries, sound turned into light and into a weightless walk through shining fields.

A few years later I stood before the Strassburg Cathedral and saluted the music-making angel floating high up in its stony splendor, a part of the architecture and yet escaping it, striving toward the ether, the home of its being and the echo of its song.

The brightness of the summer afternoon lent the towers of the cathedral a kind of unreality. And this feeling of unreality became intensified when I stepped into the church which, at first sight, did not strike me as such. There was nothing but a diffuse coolness, the light breaking in from all sides, in rays, in bundles, in pools, penetrating all matter and dissolving it in swinging motion.

And there it happened that all of a sudden I heard the long-forgotten tone again, softly, like a breath, like spun glass, unearthly, seraphic, ethereal, as if taking my hand in weightless strides: alluring, compelling, binding. That was how *Seraphic Song* came into existence in the cycle of *Shifting Landscape*. In creating it, I dealt with not only a dance idea and its thematic execution. It was mainly a matter of reducing the broadness of the theme to its most concise formula. And: such simplification must avoid turning into a poverty of ideas! Striding and floating, worship and transfiguration, all had to be carried out in equal measure. Above the spread and sound of light-flooded wings, there it had to unfold, to soar in glassy transparency, quickened by a breath which fused shape and song into oneness.

The musical form of this *Seraphic Song* was born at the very same time as its choreographic conception. It had to paint the mood and create an atmosphere equal to the message of the dance.

There were only a few widely spread chords, economically used, broadening into a kind of choral theme which underlined and clarified the restrained accents of the main motif of the dance. To brighten and extend it, the sound of the piano was joined by a glockenspiel with its seven well-attuned notes, which was the swinging and binding element that formed a harmonic dialogue, a song of the spheres between tone and movement, between dance and music.

I am unable to say how well I succeeded in materializing the image of this dance idea and in lending the gesture language, which is so very much tied to the mere physical in man, some of the transparency of those tone waves vibrating with light. And even if the artist could once succeed in bridging this last span of space that keeps man suspended between his vision and its realization, he could not be credited with it, since it would be the gift of a blessed moment which he would have to justify by honest struggle and passionate dedication to his work.

# Sacrifice

I had returned from my first American tour and was filled to the brim with all the impressions and tensions with which this so different continent had left me, with its so completely different way of living, with its different people, its noisy cities, and the vast distances of its overwhelming landscape. They were merciless months during which everything personal had to be sacrificed to one's profession. Months of struggling with and serving the dance, but also a time of triumphant victories. Only once, for the duration of a single day, was I allowed to forget all my professional duties, to surrender totally to the experience of that elemental drama which nature gave us in the creation of Niagara Falls. Later, in the quietude of my studio at home, I started to work on the choreography for *Sacrifice*. I was almost terrified by the power which compelled me to work on it. But it never entered my mind before or during this creative process to connect the choreographic theme of *Sacrifice* with my experience of seeing Niagara Falls.

From the hard struggle with this fragile theme emerged the combative *Song of the Sword*. The solemn, ceremonial *Dance for the Sun* was created. This was followed by the dark theme of *Dance into Death*, whose dramatic impact was discharged with wide gestures and space patterns. And out of a passionate lust for the instinctive play with earth-bound forces arose *Dance for the Earth*.

And then: *Lament*. It appeared like an inexplicably beautiful dream in which all pain became transfigured into deeply blissful abandonment. Seen from the choreographic viewpoint, this dance was certainly not interesting. It did not sparkle and glitter, it also did not offer any opportunity to unfold a particularly technical accomplishment. A few slow steps, a gentle bending down, and a quiet sinking to the floor — that was all. And yet I especially loved this very dance, perhaps because in its unsophisticated form it was the first step on the road to that kind of simplicity which is the desire and aim of the maturing process in any creative artist.

All these dances had a common keynote in the passionate request for: once more — one last time. And simultaneously through all these dances ran a clearly defined space line until this line, in the last dance of the cycle, *Dance into Death,* became the dominating theme of the dance form, a long diagonal cutting through the space.

I had performed *Sacrifice* more than once in public, and I was always a little afraid of this last dance. Each time before I made the first step in this, so to speak, fateful diagonal, I was gripped by an almost physical fear of the inevitability of this dance progression.

And then one day it happened after all that the imaginary curtain tore apart which until then had separated dance creation from dance experience. During my preparations for the beginning of the last dance, for this being driven into the dance diagonal, on the yet dark stage, I suddenly felt and knew with breathtaking vehemence: You experienced all this before, somewhere else, but exactly like this. And with lightning speed the images of that phenomenon of nature emerged, under whose spell I had been without knowing it.

I saw the river in front of me, streaming along so lazily and calmly in its wide bed, as if its final flow were predestined, that river which so confidently and unsuspectingly drew ever nearer to its fatal fall. I felt the crushing force of the waters next to me, above me, beneath my feet, and I remembered that little sentence which I had said to myself at the moment of the overwhelming sight of this phenomenon: The waters demand their sacrifice. . . . Thus the circle around the genesis and creation of the *Sacrifice* was completed.

SACRIFICE

DANCE FOR THE SUN

LAMENT

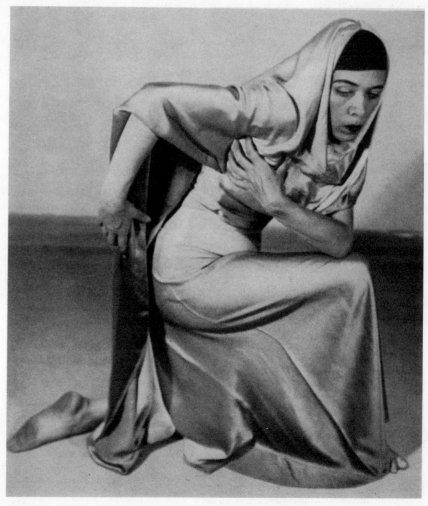

DANCE INTO DEATH

# Song of Fate

This dance was composed within a few days. But it took months before it really became *Song of Fate*. What I actually had in mind and what I felt within for a long time was a *Song of the Norns,* a dance which should have taken its place in a larger group composition, *Hymnic Dances.*

"We weave at the fabric of time." I was absolutely persecuted by this sentence, and I imagined three female figures, three ages: the young woman, the mature woman, the old woman. I saw them move, singly, by two, and by three; I felt the rhythms of their hand gestures, tying together life's thread, weaving it, and cutting it off. I was certain that these figures had to wear masks, first of all to obliterate the personalities of the dancers who were to embody them, and then, furthermore, to give the dance as such that timeless face which it had to have as I visualized it.

A gifted young sculptor wanted to carve the masks for me. As I knew from experience that you must work on such a dance with the masks from the very beginning, I waited until the masks were ready to choreograph it. They turned out to be wonderful. I looked at the mask of the young woman and knew: this is a dance-face! The second mask bearing the features of the mature woman in full bloom disturbed me. Wasn't this mask-face already too hard and bitter to justify those gestures which I imagined for this figure? And seeing the mask of the old woman, which I was to wear myself, I was terrified; because all that emerged from this face, I could not do — I could not yet do — and would probably never be able to do. The figure wearing this mask was no longer the symbol of an old woman. What looked back at me was the age-old, archaic face of a very old woman, so totally remote and removed from life that the language of this creature could only be motionless silence. This woman could no longer lift her foot, and her deadly tired hand could not even finish that last and gently symbolic action, the cutting off of the thread of life which was her destiny.

I tried again and again to move in this mask, I hoped time and again that I would finally succeed in awakening the life of dance in it. It was in vain! I had to recognize that this mask could not be put under a spell through means of the dance. And I had to abandon *Song of the Norns*.

And then it happened that *Song of Fate* rose from within me, suddenly and quite unexpectedly, out of an unbearable tension of my entire being: the hand seizing the mantle which clung to the body, stretching high, rearing up, then with three long strides into the dark and empty space, a rhythm compelling the arm to reach up — the movement theme for *Song of Fate* was born. I could hear the cry of despair within me. Behind it was the proud and defiant: "Nevertheless!," the rebellion against everything that seemed dictated by fate, hidden and unbearable; but behind it also was the humble recognition of a superior power that, wiser than myself, knew very well what was necessary and what one could bear. It was a struggle between saying Yes and saying No in which the Yes remained victorious.

I could hardly wait for the next morning when I would be able to start work, the labor of forming, shaping, composing. The dance was finished within a few days. Never had I to change anything about it. It seemed that this dance had been dormant within me, as if I just had to open myself, to give way to the creative flow, as if this dance had but waited to take on form and dance reality. Later, I asked myself whether it might have been the external situation which forced this dance to emerge, whether it was a matter of some compromise, even though a successful one. But I knew this could not have been the case. I knew that *Song of Fate* had *had* to be created.

SONG OF FATE

SONG OF FATE

AUTUMNAL DANCES

WINDSWEPT

DANCE IN THE STILLNESS

# Autumnal Dances

The cycle of *Autumnal Dances* also happened out of inner necessity. Even the title points to the experience of the season as its creative background. But why could I create these dances only in one given year? Hadn't I experienced before the fading of nature, and certainly experienced it not less intensely? And yet just at that time the autumn became a revelation to me: because this experience of nature coincided with the awareness that I myself was starting the autumn of my life. And this autumn was beautiful.

What nature wove and sang: the paean on the last flowering and ripening, the gentle reminder that everything is transitory, the brightness, the gaiety and lucidity being transfigured, the flaming splendor of the forests and the strong smell of the soil, but also the little shiver at sunset and the wild joy in the dance of the whirling leaves when the storm bends the trees, the starry nights and the deep, utterly deep silence broken by the mating call of the stag: all that sang and sounded also within me, so full, so strong, so ardent that it had to discharge itself as a hymn. That was how the first of the five autumnal dances, *Dance of Remembrance,* came into being. It actually was a thanksgiving, a salutation to the past, a farewell sent to the summer that was yet hardly gone.

How much it had given me, this summer, pouring out the cornucopia of its colors! Now it was gone, and its hot glitter started to turn into the beauty of autumnal transfiguration. Ripeness and harvest! A blessing seemed to embrace everything.

And thus the second autumnal dance also became a thanksgiving for the blessings of the earth. Was not I a part of the blessing of the great mother Nature; and blessed indeed, because life and creation were so completely in harmony with each other?

But then came a strong sound, a full chord, shaking and roaring, *Windswept,* the bride of the wind. It was wonderful once again to throw oneself into a large orbit, with the wide dance skirt swinging about, leaving the limitations of the body behind so that it swelled and billowed like a sail in the wind. How wonderful to let oneself be driven, to offer oneself enraptured — moved by the wind, wedded to the wind — to lose oneself whirling down in all the uproar like a leaf falling from a tree, to reach the ground in a last flaring up with a last faint breath. Followed by *Song of the Hunt,* starting like a fanfare — a lively 6/8 beat, with fast feet running across the floor and suddenly coming to a halt; then tensely listening and looking, statue-like — Artemis, roaming through the forests, forcing her way in great delight, imperiously sounding the hunting call which was thrown back by its echo.

As finale, *Dance in the Stillness* came — a soundless pacing, a listening-into-oneself, and a wary tracking down of all that was fading away. But, at the same time, there was a tentative groping into what the future might hold, with its covering veils only slowly lifting.

These dances were created at a time of political unrest. The anathema "degenerate art" had long since been pronounced about my work. Everything demanded utter caution. I have never known "being careful" in my work and have always gone my own way as I had to. But to this very day I ask myself how *Autumnal Dances* could remain untouched by all outside tribulations and keep their innocent purity in experience as well as creation.

# Dance of Niobe

In *Dance of Niobe* the female figure of the Greek legend came to me as the symbol of the suffering mother robbed of her growing children, one child after the other, by the god's deadly arrows.

The legend has it that she was a beautiful and proud woman, this Queen of Thebes, who was given to sun herself in the happiness of motherhood, a happiness that no other woman in the land could claim. Conceived, carried, born . . . thus they grew up, her boys and girls, in flawless beauty, overshadowing Niobe's own beauty, like young gods and goddesses. They were a royal race of her own flesh and blood through which she felt sure of immortality beyond her own life.

Who could challenge her? Didn't she have the same claim to adoration as the Olympian goddesses? And so when the women of her country, festively adorned, came to dance around the altar of the goddess of fertility and brought their sacrifices with humble love, she rebelled against it. With wanton arrogance she threw down the gauntlet before the great mother goddess: "How do you dare accept what ought to be mine? What do you have to show in deeds and offerings which are life and life-giving forces procreating time and again?"

But the goddess made a charge against Niobe and brought on her the only punishment that would hurt her hardest and in the most deadly way: the death of her innocent children.

It was not really the tragic figure of Niobe that urged me to creation. She probably was only the sketchy suggestion, only the disguise, the de-sign which made it possible for me to say what tormented and moved me so deeply: the mad arrogance, the immeasurable daring with which we — powerless and impotent — become a part of the collective guilt of having a disastrous destiny which, in its last phase, is war.

There was the terrible red night of the first terror raids. In the shelter people were crowded together, strangers, yet sharing the same fate. The two old women who had vehemently quarreled about trivialities up to the first bomb hit — now cowering hand in hand, moving their lips in soundless prayers.

Little Peter, his face aglow, accompanying every explosion with a joyous "bum-bum."

The woman, far advanced in pregnancy, her heavy belly pushed out, leaning against the wall of the cellar, gasping: "Stay with me, don't leave me alone — the child — it may come at any moment — and my husband at the front — I haven't heard from him."

Death stood behind all of us. But it had changed, lost its majesty, was only the tool of cruel wantonness which no longer acknowledged it as ruler.

We who have gone through and survived it are marked. We cannot forget it. We don't want to forget it. We must not forget it.

The agony, the misery, the grief, the fear, the restless waiting, and the sightless despair of the mothers during the war. . . . It was as if all of them wanted to drop their sorrows into my lap, urging me: "You say it, we have no voice and no tears any more!" I will never forget how this theme started to disquiet and torment me; how I caught myself again and again pressing my hands against my own body with a wary and protective gesture; how the humming of a tender lullaby was suddenly on my lips, and I was full of proud happiness, into which broke anxiety, a fear which had no name as yet until the eye opened wide in terror, the cry died in the throat, and the body, as if hit by lightning, was thrown to the ground; how the lament rose and grief yearned for the redeeming tears. How the agile arms wanted to embrace the one last child to protect it from the deadly thrust; how the clenched fists struck against my own breast in self-sacrifice: Take me, take me, but spare this one, the last child I have! Until nothing was left, nothing any more but a body which no longer belonged to me, an empty, burnt-out vessel.

Each time, when the dance was over, it seemed as if I had aged immeasurably in the few minutes of its duration and would never find my way back into life. And often before I started to dance I was overcome by a kind of timidity, never known to me up to then: wasn't it audacious to dare tackle this theme? Was its symbolically creative form pure enough and my emotional powers strong enough to soothe pain, or would I only tear open again hardly healed wounds? I wanted to call out to these grief-stricken women: Forgive me that, dancing, I sing of your pain and believe that the blood of my own heart streams out into this dance. For your grief is the grief of all of us, and it is holy to me.

DANCE OF NIOBE

FAREWELL AND THANKSGIVING

# Farewell and Thanksgiving

A tiny motif occurred to me, fleetingly, and quickly left, as do all things born of the moment.

Aleida, who accompanied me during my exercises, caught it and gave it its musical form. Now it could be done again.

It was not much, but it fitted the body as if made to measure. And every time when it re-emerged I felt as if touched by a sunbeam. A smile hovered over it, a knowing smile. Or was it a smile of resignation?

It was a dance motif of far-swinging movements, a motif of a diagonally upward fluttering gesture which sought to fade out in space, but, at an arrested instant of its suspension, was caught by the swinging leg and brought to its end in an almost imperceptible, eluding hip movement of withdrawal. Virtually, it was like a bird call, as one might hear it before dusk. Full in its sound, yet nevertheless the call of evening.

One day I found out that my motif contained enough dance substance to carry idea, structure, and development for a dance. Thus it became the basic, thematically defined pattern of the dance which I called *Farewell and Thanksgiving*.

It was the final dance of the last solo program in which I appeared before an audience.

The year was 1942. War. Traveling became troublesome. Drums and gongs had to be left at home. Also the big trunks could no longer be taken along. The costumes, always cared for with particular love, had to be packed in suitcases which could be carried more easily. Railroad sections were obstructed. Trains had to be shunted to side tracks. You sat and waited, silent and motionless. You listened with an uneasy heart to the roaring of the airplane motors, flying toward a goal unknown to you. Friend or foe? Was there such difference any longer? Those beautiful, silvery birds, actually created to span distances, to connect, to communicate! And now only tools of destruction.

It became cold in the compartments. The heating no longer functioned. There was no light. When the glimmer of the last cigarette went out, all life seemed to have died in the crowded room. It was not the cold alone that made you shiver, it was also the thought that you might no longer be able to reach your goal in time. At least, would it be possible to be there for the start of the performance?

Probably all this helped me to keep the promise I had given myself: namely, not to wait for the beginning of the decline, but to quit at the climax of my personal abilities.

I kept my promise. It was difficult. More difficult than I thought, since, after all, I was in full possession of my physical capacities. My creative forces continued to demand expression time and again and the performer, deeply rooted within me, could not be suppressed. And was it not one of the strongest and deepest feelings of happiness to be able to communicate through the art of the dance?

"Farewell and thanksgiving." . . . The dance justified what its title promised. My little motif, recurring in rhythmic intervals, lent this dance its weightlessness and that faint smile in which lies renunciation without resignation.

# Group Dance and Choric Dance

Why do I think so often these days about *Totenmal?* It lies so far back, and my thoughts have hardly ever touched upon it in all these years.

Are the questions and problems of the dispute with Sellner's staging of *Orpheus* and my choreographic contribution to it in back of it — a fact which, without my being aware of it, conjured up the images of *Totenmal,* the time of its creation, and the circumstances under which they came into being?

But what have Gluck's opera and Albert Talhoff's *Totenmal* in common with each other? One is a classical masterpiece of the musical theatre, the other an experiment of its day which very soon was buried in oblivion. The only connection which I can see between them is the fact that in both cases I did not sign alone for the production. Almost everything created before *Totenmal,* and everything — except the choreography for *Orpheus* — that came afterward, bore my personal handwriting.

1928 — the Dance Congress in Essen, where dancers from Germany and those from abroad met to test their mettle and where ballet and modern dance crossed their sharply pointed swords.

At a special performance, the Swiss poet Talhoff showed his "ritual chorus": groupings of figures which in pose and gesture were closely akin to dancing and, through a refined technique of lightning effects, were moved into an almost mystical atmosphere. Also, the possibilities for the scenic development of the dance theatre fascinated me. The consequence of this brief meeting was an exchange of letters, soon leading to a visit with Talhoff.

In the attic of his house he had put up a sorcerer's workshop. Like a magician he handled the figurines, lighting them in groups and singly and making them vanish in the darkness. They seemed to move and to be lit from inside, moved to the foreground only to fade into the spacelessness of the background where they were, lightly swaying, lifted and extinguished. Their eerie unreality was underscored by a kind of "spatial sound," produced by holding the chords of the harmonium which filled the entire room with sound.

It was impossible not to be captured by this effect! When Talhoff then began to reveal his *Totenmal* idea, I was lost. What he planned was a great choric work for dance, sound, and word in which the light — as in his "ritual chorus" — would be included in the action as a contributing factor of equal importance. However, the thought on which Talhoff's notions were founded was to create a living monument in memory of the dead of the First World War and to realize this idea through the creation and performance of *Totenmal.* — Sphere of call and countercall, sphere of oblivion, sphere of devotion! The experience of the women, of the mothers, standing still and bearing the imposed suffering, in rebellious accusation and numbed despair. The vision of the cathedral-space and its division into columns of vibrating light — the vision of misty walls cut through with rhythmically pulsating light signals. Images which, strengthened and heightened through one's own power of fantasy, virtually demanded to be created and performed by dancers. It was as if I were drawn into a cataract in whose vortex one no longer asked for the "where-to." And how Talhoff could inflame the imagination! He ignited it by setting himself ablaze. Any doubt about the possibility of the project's realization was immediately removed. Any skeptical question as to the solution of the fantastic light phenomena which ought to have permeated the whole work was nipped in the bud: "That was tried out by Zeiss in Jena a long time ago!"

Again in Dresden and surrounded by the sober worklike atmosphere of my own dance studio, I could liberate myself from the spell cast upon me by Talhoff's overwhelming intensity, I could find the necessary clarity about my task and deliberate in quietude how it could be solved. The confusing factors of the verbalization, the altars for the speakers, the rite-conducting chorus, and the narrator faded more and more into the background. What remained was the idea of the dance scenes — spacious in dimensions — which ought to take shape. And also the joyful thought remained that, for the first time, I would work in a big way; that I would gather fifty male and female dancers in order to perform with them the hymn of life and death.

Here it was, the choric task which I had struggled deep within for a long time to solve without making the final step from the group work to the chorus. Certainly, rudimentary approaches toward it were to be found in earlier works, in *Hymns in Space* and, above all, in *Celebration*.

So far this work was probably the most mature and inventive of all my group compositions. It was built symphonically throughout as pure dance, based on no connected action. Its three movements — solemn, sombre, exalted — only differed in their essential mood and contrasted in their spatial and creative forces. The first movement — called "Temple" in the program bill — consisted of four dances following one another in immediate sequence, dances whose monotonous character was based on a movement pattern in harmony with its solemn message — a kind of "ostinato" which received in each dance another nuance, another tempo, and a new variation of its basic rhythm. It was a fourfold paraphrasing of a theme which, in its totality, achieved the effect of a celebration characteristic of a cult. The solemnity was still retained in the ecstatic whirl of my *Monotony*. For here too I cast myself again as a soloist, as a single voice weaving through the whole fabric like a red thread, binding it together.

The sombre movement, *In the Sign of the Dark*, was totally attuned to the rhythmic-dynamic element. Sharply profiled groups, whose tight structure gave an almost architectonic impression, were brought to spatial solution, and so were the constantly mounting tensions through the exploitation of overrefined foot-work. The diagonal principle dominated space and was linked in the straddled leg attitude in its horizontal forward movement with knife-sharp rhythms of the feet in order to thrust high in a vertical direction with the grouping — now tearing space open, creating abysses, now filling space, towering high, only to burst it open again. It was contrapuntally built to flow into a theme composed like a fugue and to find its conclusion in total space harmony.

The costumes of the dancers corresponded with the dramatic structure arrested in its ominous darkness: a dull black, steel-gray brocade, glistening silver, and, as the only color spot, a dark-glowing burgundy red. Those were the colors. The cut of the costumes: knee-length mantles falling in wide folds from the shoulder, underlining the horizontal pattern of movement. And opposed to it were the vertically stressed figures in tight dress, barely hidden by the narrow long mantle opening in front.

To this very day I have not forgotten how impressively the dance action unfolded in its sparse color, in its almost Spartan austerity before a deep blue cyclorama draped black on both sides. And hardly ever again did I succeed in creating such absolute harmony of color, form, and line of physical and spatial rhythms as in this work.

*Festive Finale*, the third and last movement, was introduced by five dancers carrying cymbals and going to their places in sharp turns on a zigzag way. They stood there like pillars, dividing the space asymmetrically in order to introduce the festive action with the rhythmic motif of their metallic-sounding instruments.

They formed, so to speak, static moments in the light-footed airiness of movement to and fro which permeated the dance space thus created, the dancers winding around them garlandlike, circling and turning, leaping and swinging, in an exciting up-and-down of swaying vibrato which was heightened to a jubilant crescendo.

But at the beginning of each new thematic phase the static figures moved to another position, from which they ushered in the return of the varied movement sequences with the motif of their quickly repeated beats of the cymbals. How happy I was with this idea! It gave me the possibility of changing the dance space within the dance action itself and thus keeping all further action from the danger of becoming monotonous, too complex, or rigid.

Three times this change took place which, in the crescendo of its last phase, was whipped up to a fortissimo and then followed, while gradually fading out, by a pastoral theme. Rows, curves, arcs, and circles glidingly fell apart and again united the kneeling, sitting, and reclining dancers into loosely formed groups. Only a few figures emerged from it in order to surrender to the now fully widened space in fleeting encounters, in the gentle rocking of the bodies, in the lightly moving play of hands. It was the quiet after the storm in which the static figures were also a part. Then once more the call of the beating cymbals sounded. Once more the space turned into the column-formed dance area, to find its festive finale in harmony with the great jubilation of *Celebration.*

But even in this mammoth work of spatial dimension, the molding of the single figures in their interrelations superseded everything else and became solidified as the basic idea of the choric message. Only a single step from the dance group to the dance chorus! But this step was decisive and had to be made! For it was no longer a matter of the play of forces with and against one another, forces which determined the multicolored fabric of the group dance in a personal and superpersonal message. Here, the potential matter of conflict was no longer to be solved within the group itself. What was of concern here was the unification of a group of human beings into a body of movement which, representing the present and its background at the same time, strove from a unified viewpoint toward a common aim recognized by everyone; a viewpoint which no longer permitted any splitting into single actions; and which, actively participating, interfered in the conflict of fate taking place before it, or, contemplatively, took notice of this conflict in order to shift it onto the plane of recognition and experience.

Such a task asks for a certain renunciation on the part of the choreographer. It is renunciation of the ultimate exploitation of his dance material as to any special achievement of technical brilliance because the most inexorable demand of the choric principle is simplicity — in space structure, in rhythmic content, in movement, posture, and gesture, in their dynamic tensions, solutions, and crescendi. Anything that is too much, or too complicated in its detail, is an offense against the choric idea and leaves gaps which can rarely be bridged.

In the same way as the choric creation demands its antagonist — whether or not it takes actual shape or takes effect as thematic idea above and behind the events — in many cases it also asks for a leader chosen by the chorus, for the one who conveys the message powerfully, who, supported and carried by the entire chorus, advances the thematic idea and brings it to its final execution.

When I began to work on *Totenmal*, I was by no means aware of these particular demands. They made themselves felt only in the course of the creative process, and more than once I failed to recognize them. Every time it meant turning back from what was accomplished to that point where the failure had taken place. These were hard struggles which I had to fight out alone with myself, since there was no one who could have helped me.

In the scenes of *Totenmal,* two choruses opposed each other: loving women who in the torment of their loneliness advanced to the threshold of death, obsessed by the mad notion they could obliterate the finality of separation and recall the beloved in his former shape. And opposed to them the phantomlike male chorus symbolizing the dead of the war, appearing bigger than life — in staring silence, in painful, passive defense, and finally in rebellion against the women's invasion into the shadowy, twilight abode which it was no longer in their power to leave.

Well, it certainly lies within the scope of the dance to give profile and shape to the transcendental. But here I encountered fully unexpected difficulties, inhibitions which arose within me. For it was no longer a matter of conjuring up the ghostlike as such. Dignity had to be preserved, awe before the majesty of death who, even in his most incomprehensible action, remains the unimpeachable keeper of the seal within this realm.

Fear, horror, terror, pain, and despair of death — the experience of the women was burdened with all these images of war, while the male chorus stood in the realm of the forlorn and forgotten, never again to be reached by anything. There was no longer any love nor the understanding of human demands. And yet it did not suffice to force the male chorus onto a level where it would remain merely an apparition. In spite of all remoteness, in spite of the chorus being taken back into a schematic and shadowlike existence, it had to get into action, had to become the antagonist.

Time and again I could not succeed in balancing reality and superreality. Until one day I remembered that song of the Odyssey in which the great wanderer performs the expiation and blood sacrifice in order to meet the shadowy souls of the dominion of death, and, in conversation with them, to compensate for the loss of his past, suffered through his long wandering. I virtually *saw* how the shapeless shadows, while in touch with the blood — still warm with life — regained the intimation of their human features, how they became recognizable, how one could address them, yet how they remained untouchable. And though this vision could not be immediately exploited, it nevertheless kindled a little light with whose help I dared to grope forward into the inaccessible unknown.

With the exception of a single female figure — a part in which I cast myself — all *Totenmal* dancers were supposed to wear masks. Confounded, I stood in front of the fifty faces carved of wood. Could they be adjusted to the abstracting process of a dance creation? In the large-lined surface treatment of the wood, in the expression of the painfully stern defense and retreat, the male masks could be best adjusted to an almost ghostlike message. On the other hand, the torn-open faces of the women were brought into the focus of too much realism which — even though on a different level — also seemed to be forced into something phantomlike. And thus the first practical attempt failed by slipping somewhat into the grotesque. What was to be done? I knew no way out. And yet a way had to be found to come closer to these masks.

We tried it with "meditation exercises." The female dancers sat on the floor with their backs to the wall and stared at the masks lying in their laps: one minute — two minutes — five minutes. No word was spoken. Only a softly played gong melody filled the room. The same was done next evening. But that time the dancers had put the masks on their faces and observed them as reflection in mirrors which they had brought with them. This way we gradually adopted and became immersed in the style and character of the masks.

Then I began with the molding of each single figure. I had every dancer approach the large mirror in my studio in order to show where the discrepancy could be found between mask and human shape. I particularly remember the dancer wearing the mask of an old woman. The dancer's body was in utter contrast to the tormented face of the mask, furrowed with wrinkles and with the expression of one about to die. Only with utter cautiousness did I then succeed in giving the young body the gait, posture, and gesture, the imprint of the decrepitude of old age. It was an endlessly troublesome, detailed job during which I was not only concerned with bringing mask and mask-wearer into harmony with each other, but also with determining their style and with turning them into types while preserving their individual character. Only in this way could the collaboration of all in the choric message be achieved. Although it turned out that Talhoff's "light columns" could not be realized in the "cathedral-space of the call," nevertheless the first appearance of the female chorus achieved an unusually strong effect. From the dark of the background one female figure after another emerged and, for a moment, stepped into the circle of a light cone in whose intensity the figure was lit up glaringly, only to glide back into the dark again and to make room for the next figure: a young female worker, who, with hard, angular movements, relentlessly forced her way. — The blind one with the empty stare of the mask-eyes and the uncertain groping steps. — The childlike girl who, hardly yet conscious of experienced suffering, searchingly ran through space. — The mad woman in her unsteadily staggering aimlessness. — The frail old woman. — And the woman full of tears and numbed by pain, resigned and motherly kind and ready to comfort. The row of figures seemed to pass by endlessly like visions of striking strangeness.

Only thus did the women form a choric entity, in a many-divisioned procession of mourning. And there actually began my personal struggle to master the big choric structure. Every interruption of the block formation — whether or not it made room for the individual message in parallel or counter movements — had to remain a part of the total action, had to push it forward and to heighten it. Finally, lament, mourning, desire, rebellion sounded like a single scream: the desperate demand for the return of the dead. With the bodies piled upon one another and wincing in pain like wounded beasts, the female chorus changed into a huge hill of suffering above which the vision of the dead men began to dawn. Formed like an organ, pipelike, towering side by side and above one another, they appeared in the ghostly pale light of the background, and lifted slowly, incredibly slowly, the right arm in a single gesture of defense and denial.

The female chorus, however, did not hold its ground. Shaken with terror, it fell apart. And the women, now separated and lonely again, took to flight before the conjured-up apparitions of those figures which remained outside their reach. The stage was dimmed and lay there in dark silence until the speaking chorus —

built like altars to the right and left of the stage frame — commented on the dance action with questions and answers, as transition to the next scene.

The rehearsals under Talhoff's direction did not always proceed without friction. Occasionally they even led to big fights. Thus, for instance, the accompanying music, already composed in Dresden and entirely developed from the viewpoint of the dance, was rejected by him, and the dance scenes were subjected to an orchestra of sound effects which he conducted. But the dance actions, composed to the very last detail, could not bear any arbitrariness. And because of the dimensions within which they functioned, they needed a reliable support which made them independent from all other performing factors. Finally, we agreed on the metrical beating of two African drums, whose penetrating sound reached the last corner of the big stage but could not be heard in the auditorium.

It was difficult to do without the music inherent to the dance, but it proved to be the right thing. Because Talhoff's own rhythmic-melodic formulations actually were not dance-oriented. They had an explicitly picturesque sound character which would have blurred rather than underlined the clarity of the dance contours. The African drums saved us from it. Even when the broad waves of sound rolled over the stage, they could not break into the dance structure, but they seemed to surround it with a self-contained wall of sounds. The dance scenes stood up to the challenge of word and tone. Due to technical difficulties, it became necessary to dispense with the light columns, with the beat of the rhythmically directed signal lights — of whose stage effects I had expected so much; but the dance itself did not lose by it.

Too many forces, unbalanced among one another, were put into play to be able to fulfill Talhoff's wish-dream of a *Gesamtkunstwerk*. In spite of it, *Totenmal* was a unique conception, a sketch designed with grandiosity whose total effect one could not escape. The impression of the work was moving and remained so. Night after night the huge festival hall especially built for *Totenmal* was filled with people who were deeply stirred. There were those awe-inspiring moments in which, from the galleries, a few speakers read letters written by students killed in the war. Moments in which one sat there with bated breath, and sound-less weeping seemed to fill the auditorium.

There was the march of the women who, transfigured by pain, emerged from the depth of the orchestra pit in order to converse with the dead: in the sphere of forgetfulness which, at the same time, was the sphere of loving memory. It received its cemetery-like character through the figures of the male chorus: tombstones set for themselves, elevated through platforms and cothurni, as if removed into the stillness of a deep peace. No rebellion of the women this time! Ardor, humility, prayers welled up in these figures and seemed to force them to react — with a hardly noticeable turn of the head, with only a gently lifted hand. No threatening of the men. All that was left was resignation and the great mourning in recognition of the inevitable.

And there was the moment of the "counter call" in which the male chorus rose to resist the renewed penetration of their realm and to protest against war. According to Talhoff's conception, the male dancers should break open the space and fill it with the gloom of the dark as phantomlike drummers swinging flags.

The dance which came into being as a preliminary study of this task I called *Space-Shape*. It was physically so strenuous that I could take it into my solo program for only a relatively short period of time. A double strip of fabric consisting of red silk and silver-gray velvet was worked into the wide skirt of my dance costume. This strip of fabric was about thirteen feet long and was fastened on its other end to a hollow wooden stick filled with lead which lay heavily in my hands. Only this made it possible to cope with the unusual material and to master it dancewise — to throw and to swing it far through the air, to whirl it so tight around the body that it turned into a pillar, and to unfold it again in a far-reaching low movement — thus, winglike, throwing the air-and-floor-space into tumult. It was a man's job which, basically, went far beyond my strength, but which put me into a position of conveying to the dancers of *Totenmal* the execution of their task in a competent and expert manner. It would have been easy to let the last scene of *Totenmal* turn into a hellish pandemonium, into a raid of a too theatrically exploited underworld throwing itself with hatred against an animated reality and overrunning it with blind fury. But this was just what it should not be. The criterion for all the other scenes had to be applied here too: to be a memorial for the dead of the war, erected in a consecrated hour, a memento for the living and the survivors too. Once more the women set out to reach the dead. Once more entreaty and prayer flamed up together as a cry of desiring love. But then it was as if the stage would burst asunder in the dull rumbling roar of the kettledrums, in the hard beat of the drums, supported by the uninterrupted rolling thrusts of the orchestra. Formed into columns heavily stamping and almost marching on the spot, the phantomlike chorus of the men seemed to rush forward, seemed to push aside the women — who, frightened by the intensity of this vision, became motionless — seemed to level them to the ground in order to take possession of the entire realm of human experience. Above it, the crackling unfurling of the flags. Like the huge wings of the sombre angels of death, the flags swelled in the air above the heads of the dancers time and again.

Rebellion of the dead — it flamed up, it died down. Only the thunder of their steps was still audible which, growing fainter and fainter, faded in the distance and surrendered the scene to a speechless void — to a pause, to a minute of silence in which, left behind alone, I was supposed to perform the last gesture which would end *Totenmal*. Having gone through all the stages of experience of the women as the leader of the chorus, it now was my task to reconcile the sphere of the dead, which had been thrown into tumult, to return it to that quiet self-preservation which man is only justified to approach in a state of utter devotion.

From the utmost stretch of the body I glided slowly, unbelievably slowly, into the wide arc of the "bridge." In itself, there is nothing to it, it is familiar to every dancer! Only in the slow-motion deceleration, the body seemed to break to pieces and seconds turned into eternities.

Perhaps it is one of the most fascinating effects of the dance that, with its purely corporeal means, it can achieve a complete decorporealization in its message. And this was all that mattered in this last gesture. The lower the back was bent, the closer the head approached the floor and the arms — denying themselves any support — began to tremble in the air like swaying branches, the more the feeling of bodilessness took possession of me.

Devotion? Yes, but the theme to be fulfilled was already behind me. It was also painful in the transitions from one stage of depth into the other. But it was not what one generally calls "expression." There was no longer any conscious will and no possibility to enhance the personal message; there was left only the inexorable consequence of an action which, in complete self-denial, became the gesture of sacrifice. Frantically the blood was beating in my temples, my ears were buzzing, I saw black spots before my eyes. But there was never the least beginning of unconsciousness. It was rather as if one were moved into another, a supertemporal and superphysical sphere of consciousness, in which earth itself took possession of the physical existence and seemed to suck it in with a strange power of attraction — slower and yet always slower, deeper and yet always deeper. Only then when the back of the head touched the floor, the almost superhuman tension was able to loosen. The back gave in, the arms fell limp. With a deep breath I could release myself from the self-imposed spell. The lights went out. *Totenmal* had come to an end.

IN THE SIGN OF DARKNESS

TOTENMAL (IN MEMORIAM)

MOLOCH WAR

TOTENMAL (IN MEMORIAM)    THE WOMEN

CHORUS OF MEN AND WOMEN

SPACE SHAPE

# Dance Pedagogy

*Letter to a Young Dancer*

You ask many questions, my dear friend! And should I answer your questionnaire the way you wish — point after point and in form of headlines, no less — it would turn out to be what I have never wanted and do not want today: a manual, a technically oriented brochure, or even a teaching method.

No, my friend, I won't make it so easy for you. And if you would like to see in me your adviser at the beginning of your own teaching career, then you must not expect an answer to questions which almost exclusively refer to the mastering of things that are purely technical and self-understood.

After all, the mastery of a craft in all its technical and functional aspects is a prerequisite for every artistic activity. Do not forget — never forget it! — that dance-educational work is an artistically conditioned task.

Moreover, you have experienced in your own body everything that is known as dance technique. It has become second nature with you, it is what you possess. And if I may give you any advice, then let me tell you: Discover it all over again and in its living relation and immediacy from man to man.

Do you want to resign yourself to being an imitator? Speak your own language and try to convey to your students something of what drove you once to the dance: your enthusiasm, your obsession, your faith, and your relentless endurance with which you worked as a student. Have the courage to be yourself and also to help your students find the way to themselves.

But perhaps one should also speak of love, of that inner readiness which is meant for *man* in the dancer before one turns to the dancer in man — for that creature in whom everything is in ferment and rebellion, who has not yet made any final decisions, and in whom even the dancing talent has not yet come to the fore in such a way as to mean an irrevocable signpost for everything in the future.

Loving readiness — it has nothing to do with the love of the teacher for his student as an individual, and certainly nothing to do with that romantic love for mankind and one's fellowman which befools and befogs, which creates confusion instead of clarity and returns like a boomerang where it started from because, in reality, it is concerned with one's own self.

One could rather speak of the "pedagogic Eros," of that fluctuating condition of belonging in which human movement and artistic obligation meet on the level of a living exchange; and student and teacher circle — in a constantly renewed movement toward and away from each other — around the one center which, in our case, is called "dance."

You ask about the secret of pedagogic success. And I ask in turn: Does it exist at all? If the teacher were to credit himself for success and recognition of his student, he would not be a pedagogue.

You had better ask for the secret of a pedagogic talent. It is, like every other talent, a gift which you can neither earn nor achieve through work, of course; a gift which obliges its owner to a far-reaching extent because it imposes a responsibility upon him which goes beyond himself and involves other human beings. What would artistic creativity be if the secret of selection did not exist! Why was talent bestowed upon one person and refused to someone else?

We try to explain everything. And almost anything can be explained. If we no longer succeed in it in our trade jargon, a simile may help us along. But when one believes that everything is said and made lucid, one then hits upon a point behind which the big question marks emerge, behind which ideas and images gradually become veiled and everything that can be taught and learned is replaced by that which can only be surmised.

Where does it come from, this joy to shape and form, the love of the gardener for living growth? Does not the desire to teach — in fact the necessity to do it! — originate in the same source from which flows the impulse leading to artistic creativity? They may arise from quite different layers. But is not the same relentless urge to communicate behind it, and the just as relentless urge to create?

I can only see dance education as a formative task above and beyond which, as its strongest accent, the human being is placed in all his corporeality.

Is it then forming the body? Yes — for it is a matter of a growing process in which physical movement, spiritual agility, and mental versatility must be balanced in order to achieve the transformation of the physical in man to the body as instrument. To reveal the whole range of movement potentialities to the young dancer, to bring him close to a fulfilled message which sounds like a fully flowing chord — that is what matters. In a certain way it is a sculptor's work in which, under the watchful eye of the pedagogue, the moving body is turned into a sensitively vibrating and perfectly mastered instrument of the dance; into a vessel lighting up in its transparency, reflecting the agitating and moving content of the dance in a harmonious orchestration; and into the condensation of purified form. That is it! And to strive for it — and if possible also to achieve it — is task and aim which teacher and student have to solve and accomplish together in tacit agreement.

A wonderful adventure, fascinating discoveries during which you assist your student year in year out, always being the same again in always new content and changed shape. I have now practiced it for almost fifty years and have never tired of it.

Every beginning is difficult, but every beginning is also beautiful. How I love the first stammering disclosures which the young person wrests from his body, yet unconcerned with and unburdened by the problems of bodily movement and danced message, of rhythmic-dynamic rules and analytic-functional realization. Don't deprive your students of the expression of their first beginnings! For in them you will find yourself. And here you learn about them in the best and quickest way, because here they tell of themselves and say the truth.

Pupils come and go. You accept them, and just when they start to stand more securely on their own feet, you let them go again. This is the pedagogic fate. Do not expect any gratitude from your students, my friend! They are much too much occupied with themselves to comprehend and fully realize how they were guided and what they have received. The gratitude, the consciously paid tribute, come ten years later. You can be sure of that.

Teach your students to see and to absorb with waking eyes the manifold eventfulness of their everyday life. It has more to say and to give than one may think to perceive just in passing by. Teach them to think in terms of big dimensions. The spatial relationships do not tolerate any narrow-minded limitations. They demand a spiritual expansion in the same degree in which the dance gesture strives for faraway space.

Teach your students to work, concentrated and indefatigable. Strengthen them in the struggle to be hard on themselves. The dance profession is inexorable in its demands, and the young dancer has no time to lose. As far as he is concerned, the time of his ability to perform is brief and limited. He can survive himself, but he can't put his work on ice in order to start it again after many a year fresh and ready for use. Time has passed him by.

Patience is necessary, my friend, a great deal of patience — and do not forget the humor which, better than any other means, is able to brighten those dark moments in which the relationship between teacher and student begins to stiffen over an unsolved teaching problem. A liberating laughter purifies the air and immediately restores the normal process of the work.

Of course some judgment of human beings belongs with it — and a gentle hand which, in almost unnoticeable guidance, contributes to the formative growth of the young human being.

To give lessons and to teach are not always the same, and a good trainer is not necessarily a pedagogue too. Analysis and the control of movement processes are a part of the craft and are the dancer's daily bread.

But to teach means to shed light on the teaching material from all sides, to convey it from the aspects of the functional as much as from the viewpoint of spiritual penetration and emotional experience.

The dance is not an everyday language, although its material is the same movement of which man avails himself in his everyday expression. Dance is, like poetry and music, the intense concentration of uncountable oscillations striving toward one another in order to crystallize into the growing and molding of form. And that which is "between the lines" characterizes the form not less than anything that is clearly expressed. Even in the naked purity of the abstract gesture, the spiritual and mental background flows along in a vibrating innuendo and gives it a special flavor and color in the interplay of light and shadow through which the dance creation lives in space and grows into an artistic experience. It is wonderful when the sweat of work runs down steaming bodies, when faces burn, when physical accomplishment goes beyond everything one thought possible and exertion turns into joy.

But I have also experienced how a group of young people begins to glow from within and to emit a radiant power in which everything physical is suspended and gives way to a spiritualization which lifts the dance creation onto the level of enchantment and transfiguration.

"A foot that smiles, a hand that can weep" — well, the dance is not only an art of time and space, it also is the art of the consciously lived and fulfilled moment, not different in the studio from onstage. The division of the teaching program in the study of posture and movement, of space and structure, has validity merely as a principle of order. Because where only one of the elementary qualities is missing, the whole thing is no longer right. For yourself and your students, keep your senses open for the experience of the creative moment in which the well of life bubbles.

Let nothing be said against virtuosity! We expect it from any dancer of stature. But the dancer who is brilliant in nothing else but in the splendor of sheer technique and who whirls around onstage in a mechanistic vacuum does not belong among those who are "chosen." And those others who, in narcissistic self-reflection, always refer to themselves only, and no longer notice that they move on a mirrorlike plane of solitude in which no living being can go on breathing — they, too, have been denied the divine spark. They block their own way.

And here we encounter the limitations of any possible pedagogic effectiveness. For here nature is at work and lets no one wrest its secret from it.

Certainly we are able to do a great deal when it comes to molding and forming, to furthering and developing. But it is not in our power to create the often hotly desired great talent. We are not even able to determine the degree and kind of talent. For if nature has not planted the fuel of artistic talent in man, no power, no desire, no will is able to ignite the torch to that flaming light in which the creative force can give of itself lavishly, in which the language of dance finds its heightened expression in a *work of art* and the dancer becomes the carrier and messenger of the *art of dancing*. Talent is a blessing. And so is the pedagogic talent in dance. Our task, however, lies in serving: to serve the dance, to serve the work, to serve man, and to serve life.

Keep the artistic fire from being extinguished, dear friend — hold high the torch!

M.W.

Mary Wigman's

choreographed and publicly performed dance works

1914–1961

SOLO DANCES

| 1914 | Witch Dance I |
| | Lento |
| | A Day of Elves |

| 1917 | The Tumbler of Our Lady |

| 1918/19 | Marche Orientale   Scherzo |
| | Serenade |
| | Yaravi |

Ecstatic Dances
1. Prayer      3. Idolatry
2. Sacrifice   4. Temple Dance

Four Hungarian Dances (based on Brahms)
Eroica
Waltz

| 1920 | Polonaise (Liszt) |
| | Dance Suite (Dvořak) |

1. Prelude      3. Waltz
2. Play         4. Allegro con brio

Four Dances based on Oriental Motifs
1. Arabesque   3. Sign
2. Soaring     4. Center

Dances of the Night
a. Shadow
b. Dream

The Spook
Vision

SOLO DANCES

1920/23 Dance Rhythms I a. Triste
          b. The Call

     Dance Rhythms II a. Song of the Sword
            b. Lament
            c. Zamacueca

1920/23 Suite in Old Style 1. Polonaise
           2. Gavotte
           3. Sarabande
           4. Rigadoon

     Spanish Suite  1. Canción
           2. Allegro airoso
           3. Malagueña

     Two Dances of Silence

     Dance Sequence of Russian Songs

     The Cry
     The Road

     Variations on a Heroic Theme

     Two More Dances for the Spanish Suite
           a. Romance
           b. Seguidilla

1923/24 Appassionato
     Two Dance Songs
     Two Dance Rhythms

GROUP DANCES

1920/23 Works for solo and little groups
     Celebration I:  1. Greetings
           2. Spell
           3. Consecration
           4. Chant

1920/23 Dance Suite (Bizet):
           1. Intermezzo
           2. Minuet
           3. Farandole

     Dance Macabre (Saint-Saëns)
     Grotesque
     Two Dance Rhythms
     Flight

     The Seven Dances of Life
     Dance poem for solo and little group by Mary
     Wigman. Music: Heinz Pringsheim. World
     Premiere: Opera House, Frankfurt/Main
     Dance Sequence:  Prelude
            Dance of Longing
            Dance of Love
            Dance of Lust
            Dance of Sorrow
            Dance of the Demon
            Dance of Death
            Dance of Life

1923/24 Works for large groups
     Single Dances:  March
            Polonaise I
            Rhapsody II (Liszt)
            Polonaise II
            Silhouettes (Arensky)

| SOLO DANCES | GROUP DANCES |
|---|---|
| | |

**SOLO DANCES**

1923/24   Final Dance of the Rhapsody (Liszt)
                     a. Alla marcia
                     b. All'improvisato
                     c. Allegretto zingarese

1924   Dances in the Evening (Three Elegies)

1925   Two More Dances for the Spanish Suite

       For the Sequence of "Visions"
             Vision   I  Ceremonial Figure
             Vision  II  Masked Figure
             Vision III  Spectre

1926   Festive Prelude
       Rhapsodic Dance
       Two Monotonies    a. Restrained
                             b. Turning
       For the Sequence of "Visions"
             Vision IV  Witch Dance
             (Mask Dance)

1927   Dance Song for Celebration II

       Bright Oscillations
                 1. With a Big Verve
                 2. Tender Flowing
                 3. Playful

       For the Sequence of "Visions"
             Vision V  Dream Figure

       Four Dances based on Songs from the Balkans

**GROUP DANCES**

1923/24   Scenes from a Dance Drama
                  1. Summons
                  2. Wandering
                  3. Circle
                  4. Triangle
                  5. Chaos
                  6. Turn
                  7. Vision
                  8. Encounter
                  9. Salute

1925   Group Song

       A Dance Fairy Tale
            Figures:  The Moon
                     Three Girls Transformed
                        into Flowers
                     The Youth
                     The Guards
                     The Great Demon
                     The Magician
                     The Master Magician
                     The Drummers

1926   Dance of Death (Mask Dance)

       Hymns in Space
                 1. Festive Prelude
                 2. Swinging Row
                 3. The Ray
                 4. Rhythm

| SOLO DANCES | GROUP DANCES |
|---|---|
| 1927   Ballad I<br>For the Sequence of "Visions"<br>     Vision VI   Ceremonial Figure<br>     Vision VII   Ghostly Figure | 1926   Suite to Russian Folk Songs and Rhythms<br>     1. Dark Train<br>     2. The Block<br>     3. Dance Song<br>     4. Variations on a<br>        Rhythmic Theme |
| 1928   For the Sequence of "Visions"<br>     Vision VIII  Space Shape<br>         (Study for Totenmal) | 1927   Celebration II (first version)<br>     Part 1:  The Temple<br>     Part 2:  In the Sign of Darkness<br>     Part 3:  a. Polonaise<br>           b. Dance Song<br>           c. Tarantella |
| 1929   Shifting Landscape (cycle)<br>     1. Invocation<br>     2. Seraphic Song<br>     3. Face of Night<br>     4. Pastoral<br>     5. Festive Rhythm<br>     6. Dance of Summer<br>     7. Storm Song<br><br>     Gypsy Dances (Three Dance Songs) | 1928   Celebration (final version)<br>     Part 1:  The Temple<br>           (Four Monotonies)<br>     Part 2:  In the Sign of Darkness<br>     Part 3:  Festive Finale |
| 1930   Dance of Grief | 1929   Choric Movement (Three Studies) |
| 1931   Sacrifice (cycle)<br>     1. Song of the Sword<br>     2. Dance for the Sun<br>     3. Death Call<br>     4. Dance for the Earth<br>     5. Lament<br>     6. Dance into Death | 1930   Totenmal<br>Staging and rehearsing of the dramatic dance scenes based on the poem and total score by Albert Talhoff. Creation of the leading dance figure |
|      Polonaise<br>     Rondo | 1932   The Road (cycle)<br>     1. Heroic Chord<br>     2. Nocturnal Song<br>        (solo M.W.)<br>     3. Dream Birds<br>     4. Shadows (threatening<br>        and fleeing shadows)<br>     5. Pastoral |
|      Four Dances based on Hungarian Folk Songs |      6. Heroic Finale |

| SOLO DANCES | GROUP DANCES |
|---|---|
| **1934** Maternal Dance<br>Dance of Silent Joy<br>(for the cycle "Women's Dances") | **1934** Women's Dances (cycle)<br>    1. Wedding Dance<br>      (in three parts)<br>    2. Maternal Dance<br>    3. Lament for the Dead<br>    4. Dance of Silent Joy<br>    5. Prophetess<br>    6. Witch Dance |
| **1935** Song of Fate<br>Moon Song<br>(for the cycle "Dance Songs") | **1935** Hymnic Dances<br>    1. Paean<br>    2. Song of Fate<br>    3. Road of the Supplicant<br>    4. Moon Song<br>    5. Dance of Fire<br>    6. Dance of Homage |
| **1937** Autumnal Dances (cycle)<br>    1. Dance of<br>      Remembrance<br>    2. Blessing<br>    3. Windswept<br>    4. Hunting Song<br>    5. Dance in the Stillness | **1936** Lament for the Dead<br>Large chorus staged for the Festival of the<br>Youth-Olympics, Berlin, Olympia Stadium |
| **1938/41** Ballad II<br>Play<br>Dance of the Queen of Light<br>Dance of the Queen of Night<br>The Call<br>Three Dances to Polish Folk Songs<br>Dialogue | **1943** Choreography and scenic arrangement of<br>Orff's "Carmina Burana" |
| **1942** Be Calm, My Heart<br>Rejoice, My Heart<br>Dance of Brunhild<br>Dance of Niobe<br>Farewell and Thanksgiving<br><br>Mary Wigman concludes her career as a solo<br>dancer | **1946** Three Choric Studies<br>  of the Misery of Time<br>    1. Escape<br>    2. Those Seeking<br>    3. In Loving Memory<br>Performed by students of the Wigman School,<br>Leipzig<br><br>**1947** Staging and choreography of the opera<br>"Orpheus and Eurydice" by Gluck<br>Municipal Opera, Leipzig |

117

1952    Choric Studies:    Those Waiting

The Homeless

Grievance and Accusation

Performed by students of the Mary Wigman
Studio, Berlin

1953    Group Dances:

Farewell-Sarabande

(based on Honegger)

Lament for Orpheus

(based on Stravinsky)

Ecstatic Rhythm (based on Honegger)

Maenad's Rhythm (based on Borries)

Mary Wigman Studio, Berlin

Choric Scenes:    1. The Prophetess

2. The Temple

3. The Street

a. Twilight

b. Resounding Steps

c. Danger

d. Spook

4. The Road

Mary Wigman Studio Berlin
Productions: Berlin and Festival Recklinghausen

1954    Staging and choreography of the oratorio
"Saul" by Haendel
National Theatre, Mannheim

1955    Staging and choreography of "Catulli
Carmina" and "Carmina Burana" by Orff
National Theatre, Mannheim

1957    Staging and choreography of "Le Sacre du
Printemps" by Stravinsky
Municipal Opera, Berlin, Berlin Festivals

1958    Staging and choreography of the opera
"Alcestis" by Gluck
National Theatre, Mannheim

1961    Choreography for the opera "Orpheus and
Eurydice" by Gluck as staged by G. R. Sellner
German Opera, Berlin, Berlin Festivals